FOIA IN THE 21ST CENTURY: USING TECHNOLOGY TO IMPROVE TRANSPARENCY IN GOVERNMENT

HEARING

BEFORE THE

SUBCOMMITTEE ON TECHNOLOGY, INFORMATION
POLICY, INTERGOVERNMENTAL RELATIONS AND
PROCUREMENT REFORM

OF THE

COMMITTEE ON OVERSIGHT
AND GOVERNMENT REFORM

HOUSE OF REPRESENTATIVES

ONE HUNDRED TWELFTH CONGRESS

SECOND SESSION

MARCH 21, 2012

Serial No. 112–140

Printed for the use of the Committee on Oversight and Government Reform

Available via the World Wide Web: http://www.fdsys.gov
http://www.house.gov/reform

U.S. GOVERNMENT PRINTING OFFICE

74–376 PDF · WASHINGTON : 2012

For sale by the Superintendent of Documents, U.S. Government Printing Office
Internet: bookstore.gpo.gov   Phone: toll free (866) 512–1800; DC area (202) 512–1800
Fax: (202) 512–2104   Mail: Stop IDCC, Washington, DC 20402–0001

CONTENTS

FOIA IN THE 21ST CENTURY: USING TECHNOLOGY TO IMPROVE TRANSPARENCY IN GOVERNMENT

WEDNESDAY, MARCH 21, 2012,

House of Representatives,
Subcommittee on Technology,
Committee on Oversight and Government Reform,
Washington, D.C.

The subcommittee met, pursuant to notice, at 3:16 p.m. in room 2154, Rayburn House Office Building, the Honorable Mike Kelly [chairman of the subcommittee], presiding.

Present: Representatives Kelly, Chaffetz, Walberg, Lankford, Meehan, Farenthold, Lynch, Connolly, Murphy and Speier.

Staff Present: Kurt Bardella, Majority Senior Policy Advisor; Michael R. Bebeau; Molly Boyl, Majority Parliamentarian; Gwen D'Luzanksy, Majority Assistant Clerk; Adam P. Fromm, Majority Director of Member Services and Committee Operations; Justin LoFranco, Majority Director of Digital Strategy; Tegan Millspaw, Majority Research Analyst; Mary Pritchau, Majority Professional Staff Member; Laura L. Rush, Majority Deputy Chief Clerk; Peter Warren, Majority Legislative Policy Director; Jaron Bourke, Minority Director of Administration; Krista Boyd, Minority Deputy Director of Legislation/Counsel; Ashley Etienne, Minority Director of Communications; Adam Koshkin, Minority Staff Assistant; Suzanne Owen, Minority Health Policy Advisor; Rory Sheehan, Minority New Media Press Secretary; and Cecelia Thomas, Minority Counsel.

Mr. KELLY. This is a hearing on FOIA in the 21st Century: Using Technology to Improve Transparency in Government.

The hearing will come to order.

This is the Oversight Committee's Mission Statement. We exist to secure two fundamental principles. First, Americans have a right to know that the money Washington takes from them is well spent. Second, Americans deserve an efficient, effective government that works for them.

Our duty on the Oversight and Government Reform Committee is to protect these rights. Our solemn responsibility is to hold government accountable to taxpayers because taxpayers have a right to know what they get from their government.

We will work tirelessly in partnership with citizen watchdogs to deliver the facts to the American people and bring genuine reform to the Federal bureaucracy. This is the mission of the Oversight and Government Reform Committee.

(1)

I am going to allow myself an opening statement.

Today's hearing is going to address the transparency in government and how advances in technology can be used to improve public access to information. This hearing will focus particularly on the Freedom of Information Act, or FOIA, which is the primary tool the public has to get information from their government.

Transparency is extremely important and is necessary in order to have a government that is accountable to its people. Holding the government accountable and ensuring the public's right to know represents the fundamental mission of this Committee.

When President Obama took office, one of his first actions was to release a new memo on FOIA directing agencies to adopt a presumption of openness and in a statement to the public, the President said "Transparency and the rule of law will be the touchstone of this presidency." I would like to now play a short clip of his comments.

[Video shown.]

Mr. KELLY. Those are very strong words. I completely agree with President Obama's statements. However, during last week's Sunshine in Government Week, many transparency groups expressed concern with this Administration's compliance with FOIA. These concerns address a variety of issues including agency stonewalling, delays and excessive fees. Recently, the Central Intelligence Agency had a class action lawsuit filed against it for illegally discouraging requests by imposing significant fees without notifying requestors.

The Department of Homeland Security has also been accused of charging exorbitant fees on FOIA requests. During this Committee's review of agency FOIA logs, we found one case where the agency charged the requestor over $70,000.

The Department of Justice, which is responsible for setting agency FOIA compliance, has also been accused of defending Federal agencies when they choose to withhold documents. Last year when asked by the Supreme Court about President Obama's presumption of openness, the Department of Justice lawyer said, "We do not embrace that principle."

Clearly, there is more work to be done to ensure that citizens get prompt and substantive responses to their requests for government information. Technology is valuable tool for promoting transparency and is the focus of our hearing today.

I look forward to hearing from our witnesses about ways to make government more transparent and more accountable to the public.

Mr. KELLY. I now recognize the distinguished Ranking Member, Mr. Connolly, for his opening statement.

Mr. CONNOLLY. I thank the distinguished Chairman.

As I said before, my great grandfather Kelly would be proud that there was a Kelly sitting in that chair. He would be even prouder if there was his great grandson sitting in that chair, but that is a different issue.

We are delighted to have you all here today. I agree with the distinguished Chairman the first part of everything said and I disagree with the second part of everything he said. I actually believe there is a record of enormous transparency that is unprecedented in the Obama Administration. I actually believe this Committee, despite its best efforts, has actually allowed that to be documented.

Last year, for example, the full Committee held a hearing on FOIA and, hyperbole and rhetoric aside, we discussed several FOIA advancements since 2009. First, the President issued the Executive Order the distinguished Chairman referred, directing agencies to err on the side of disclosure rather than secrecy, a reversal, I might add, of the Bush era policy, which certainly favored secrecy led by the distinguished Vice President, at the time, Dick Cheney.

Second, agencies reduced the FOIA backlog, this is a fact, by 40 percent, eliminating 55,000 backlogged FOIA requests, an accomplishment by any measure. At the time, President Obama had only been in office two years. Last year, the number of FOIA requests increased dramatically and yet, 23 of 37 agencies, more than half, still managed to reduce their backlog. Unfortunately, over 250,000 new requests submitted to the Department of Defense and the Department of Homeland Security increased the government-wide FOIA backlog.

While most agencies improved FOIA management substantially, it seems some could still learn from the best practices of others. To that end, I appreciate the EPA witness appearing at today's hearing to discuss its FOIA Module web portal. The EPA's portal, which works with multiple agencies, helps the public submit and track FOIA requests, search for information and view agency responses to FOIA requests. It allows agency employees to log in securely and to process applications.

From relatively modest, upfront and annual operating costs, this portal allows EPA to save approximately $3.5 million over a five year period. This sufficient return on investment should encourage other agencies to consider adopting similar modules to achieve similar savings and efficiencies.

Similarly, agencies are unlikely to be able to reduce FOIA backlogs or provide quality FOIA responses, a metric that is every bit as important as speed of responding if agencies are subjected to arbitrary reductions in the size of their workforce. We cannot have it both ways up here, Mr. Chairman. We cannot complain about the responsiveness on FOIA requests while we are hacking away at the Federal workforce and disparaging Federal employees in the process. We cannot allow antipathy toward the Federal Government to impair our ability to respond to citizens' needs. The Office of Personnel Management projects that retirements will increase some 18 percent next year alone. In addition to understanding potential technology improvements for FOIA, we need to recognize staffing needs as well.

I want to thank the witnesses for appearing today and I look forward to learning especially more about EPA's module to see how we can save money and perhaps help other agencies.

Thank you, Mr. Chairman, for holding this hearing.

Mr. KELLY. I thank my Irish colleague. I cannot say what my grandfather would have wished. There are more Kelly's and Connolly's than we can possibly keep track of.

We are going to recognize right now our first panel: Ms. Melanie Ann Pustay, Director, Office of Information Policy, U.S. Department of Justice; Ms. Miriam Nisbet, Director, Office of Government Information Services, National Archives & Records Administration;

and Mr. Andrew Battin, Director, Office of Information Collection, Environmental Protection Agency. Thank you all for being here.

Pursuant to Committee rules, all witnesses must be sworn before they testify. Please rise and raise your right hands.

Do you solemnly swear or affirm that the testimony you are about to give will be the truth, the whole truth, and nothing but the truth?

[Witnesses respond in the affirmative.]

Mr. KELLY. May the record reflect that all witnesses answered in the affirmative. You may be seated.

In order to allow time for discussion, if you could, please limit your testimony to five minutes. We won't be real strict on that, but if you could, that would be great. Your entire written statement will be made a part of the record.

Ms. Pustay, would you please open?

WITNESS

STATEMENT OF MELANIE ANN PUSTAY

Ms. PUSTAY. Good afternoon, Chairman Kelly, Ranking Member Connolly, and members of the Subcommittee.

I am pleased to be here today to discuss agency use of technology in administering the Freedom of Information Act and the Department of Justice's continuing efforts to ensure that President Obama's "Memo on the FOIA," as well as Attorney General Holder's "FOIA Guidelines," are fully implemented.

The Attorney General issued his new FOIA Guidelines during Sunshine Week three years ago and based on our review of Chief FOIA Officer reports and agency annual FOIA reports, it is clear that agencies are continuing to make significant, tangible progress in implementing the guidelines and expanding their use of technology to do so.

In fiscal year 2011, despite being faced with a noticeable increase in the number of incoming requests, agencies were able to process over 30,000 more requests than the previous year. The government released records in response to 93 percent of requests where records were located and processed for disclosure, marking the third straight year in which such a high release rate was achieved. The government also improved its average processing time for simple requests.

Agencies continue to meet the demand for public information by proactively posting information on their websites. Many agencies have also taken steps to make those websites more useful by redesigning them, by adding enhanced search capabilities and by utilizing online portals and dashboards that facilitate access to information.

For example, the Department of Energy created a full text, searchable FOIA portal that provides access to documents previously released under FOIA. Similarly, numerous components of the Department of Defense made improvements to their websites and created systems for the proactive posting of contracts.

I am particularly proud to report on the successes achieved by the Department of Justice. For the second straight year, DOJ maintained a record high 94.5 percent release rate for those requests where records were processed for disclosure. Perhaps even more significant, when the Department released records, it did so in full in response to 79 percent of requests. Despite three straight years of receiving over 60,000 requests, the Department also increased the number of requests processed and reduced our backlog by 26 percent.

My office carries out the Department's statutory responsibilities to encourage compliance with the FOIA. As part of our work in implementing the Attorney General's Guidelines and our commitment to the initiatives in the National Action Plan for the Open Government Partnership, OIP is leading the effort to maximize the use of technology across Federal agencies to streamline the FOIA process and to improve the online availability of information.

Just this past year, OIP reconvened the Interagency FOIA Technology Working Group to exchange ideas on this important topic. The group discussed various tools to assist with FOIA processing, including technology that can aid in the search and review of documents, shared platforms that allow for simultaneous review and comment on documents, and software that automatically identifies duplicative material.

An area that I believe holds great promise in increasing the efficiency of agency FOIA processes is the use of litigation software in the FOIA context. Agencies often have to manually review hundreds, if not thousands, of pages of paper and electronic records for both responsiveness and duplication before disclosure analysis can even be made.

By utilizing e-discovery tools to perform some of these necessary administrative tasks, agency FOIA staff can focus their efforts on reviewing records for disclosure and providing a timely response. OIP has already begun using this technology and we will continue to develop its capability with the goal of helping all agencies employ similar tools for the overall benefit of FOIA administration.

We are also researching new technologies that will substantially improve the FOIA consultation process by allowing multiple components and agencies to review and comment on material simultaneously.

With well over 1 million visitors since we launched last March, the Department's new government-wide FOIA website, FOIA.gov, has revolutionized the way FOIA data is made available to the public and has become a valuable resource for both requestors and agencies. The website graphically displays the detailed statistics contained in annual FOIA reports and allows users to compare data between agencies in overtime. The website also serves as an educational resource by providing useful information about how the FOIA works, where to make requests and what to expect through the FOIA process.

Recently we expanded the function of the site even further by adding a new search tool that will help the public locate information that is already available on Federal Government websites. This new tool allows the public to enter a search term on any topic of interest and FOIA.gov will then search across all government websites at once and then capture documents posted anywhere on an agency website.

We launched yet another new feature just a few weeks ago by including hyperlinks to the on-line request forms that agencies have to make it easier than ever to make a FOIA request. In an effort to improve FOIA processes and increase efficiency, there are over 100 offices across the government that have already developed the capability to receive requests online.

I am very pleased to report that OIP itself, my office, has just launched an online capability. Requestors can now make requests and file administrative appeals online. Our portal also allows the public to establish their own user accounts and they can track the status of their request or appeal at any time and receive their determination from OIP through the portal.

Looking ahead, we will continue to work on administration of the FOIA and to enhance government transparency. We will be looking to explore new ways to utilize technology to achieve these goals. We look forward to working with the Committee on these important matters.

Thank you.

[Prepared statement of Ms. Pustay follows:]

Testimony of Melanie Ann Pustay,

Director of the Office of Information Policy

United States Department of Justice

Good afternoon Chairman Lankford, Ranking Member Connolly, and Members of the

Subcommittee. I am pleased to be here today to discuss agencies' use of technology in

administering the Freedom of Information Act (FOIA) and the Department of Justice's continued

efforts of the past year to ensure that President Obama's January 21, 2009 Memorandum on the

FOIA, as well as Attorney General Holder's FOIA Guidelines, are fully implemented. As the

lead federal agency responsible for implementing the FOIA across the government, the

Department of Justice is strongly committed to encouraging compliance with the Act by all

agencies and to promoting open government.

The Attorney General issued his new FOIA Guidelines during Sunshine Week three years

ago, on March 19, 2009. The Guidelines address the presumption of openness that the President

called for in his FOIA Memorandum, the necessity for agencies to create and maintain an

effective system for responding to requests, and the need for agencies to proactively and

promptly make information available to the public. Stressing the critical role played by agency

Chief FOIA Officers in improving FOIA performance, the Attorney General called on all Chief

FOIA Officers to review their agencies' FOIA administration each year and to report to the

Department of Justice on the steps taken to achieve improved transparency. These Chief FOIA

Officer Reports were completed last week for the third time since the Attorney General's FOIA

Guidelines were issued.

The Chief FOIA Officer Reports have become an invaluable tool for assessing agency implementation of the FOIA Guidelines. Each year they have also illustrated the broad array of activities agencies have undertaken, including the use of new technologies, to improve their administration of the FOIA and to improve transparency overall. This past year, the Department of Justice directed agencies to address new questions in their Chief FOIA Officer Reports that build on the successes of the 2011 Reports. For example, in addition to asking agencies to describe their efforts to make information available on agency websites, for 2012, we asked agencies to also address any steps that had been taken to make that posted information more useful to the public. Based on our review of both the Chief FOIA Officer Reports and agency Annual FOIA Reports, it is clear that agencies continue to make real progress in applying the presumption of openness, improving the efficiency of their FOIA processes, reducing their backlogs of pending FOIA requests, making more information available proactively and expanding their use of technology. While there is always more work to be done, for the third year in a row, agencies have shown that they are improving FOIA compliance and increasing transparency.

In Fiscal Year 2011, agencies were faced with an increase in the number of incoming FOIA requests, which rose from 597,415 in Fiscal Year 2010 to 644,165 in Fiscal Year 2011. Notably, the Department of Homeland Security experienced a 35% increase in the number of incoming requests. Overall, agencies were able to increase the number of requests that they processed in Fiscal Year 2011, increasing the number of processed requests by 30,575. Most significantly, when agencies processed those requests they increased the amount of material that was provided to the requester. Indeed, the government released records in full or in part in response to 93.1% of requests where records were located and processed for disclosure. This marks the third straight year in which the government achieved such a high release rate. This sustained, high release rate is a tribute to the efforts of FOIA professionals across the government as they work tirelessly to apply the FOIA Guidelines to the hundreds of thousands of requests they process throughout the year.

Agencies also continue to meet the demand for public information by proactively posting information of interest to the public. For example, the Department of Education annually receives more than 700 requests for contracts, grant applications, and information about federally funded programs. Through efforts to proactively identify these records and post them online, the Department of Education increased the amount of material it proactively disclosed in its FOIA Library by 25%. The Department of Homeland Security increased the amount of information it proactively released by 43%, posting nearly nine thousand pages of new information on its website. Similarly, the Department of State added over two thousand documents to its online Rwandan Declassification Collection. Within a day of issuing the long-awaited accident report for the 2010 Upper Big Branch mining disaster, the Department of Labor's Mine Safety and Health Administration posted a substantial amount of supporting data that was considered in the report, including nearly 30,000 pages of interview transcripts.

In addition to proactively posting new information, many agencies have also taken steps to make the information on their websites more useful to the public. Several agencies undertook efforts this past year to redesign their websites to make them more user-friendly and to improve their websites' search capabilities. For example, the Department of Energy recently consolidated and upgraded several websites into a new department-wide website, which utilizes interactive maps and graphics to display information in a more accessible format and allows users to search for documents and resources using a single search engine. Agencies are also utilizing online portals and dashboards to facilitate access to information. For example, the Department of Energy created a FOIA portal that is full-text searchable and provides access to documents previously released under the FOIA. The Department of Agriculture added material to its Tribal Institutions Portal to provide information on applying for and managing grants. The Department of Transportation's Federal Aviation Administration launched a new online dashboard to provide the public with information on the modernization of air transportation system infrastructure, and its Federal Motor Carrier Safety Administration is publishing information through an Application Program Interface. Numerous components of the Department of Defense made improvements to their websites, created systems to facilitate the proactive posting of contracts, and used social media to educate the public in real time about vital information on available programs and resources, such as those relating to traumatic brain injury. The Department of Health and Human Services' Administration for Children and Families has installed a live chat feature on the website of its Child Welfare Information Gateway, through which users can engage with an Information Specialist who will assist with questions, concerns, or trouble locating information. The Environmental Protection Agency is developing a potentially promising pilot -- which we are watching with interest-- for its existing FOIA solution. We understand this new tool is expected to have additional functionality that will allow the public to make, track and receive responses to FOIA requests online, will contain an online repository of previously answered FOIA requests, and will enable production of an Annual FOIA Report.

Embracing the President's FOIA Memorandum and the Attorney General's Guidelines, many agencies have gone beyond using their websites to disseminate information of public interest and have increasingly utilized social media tools such as blogs, Twitter, Facebook, and YouTube to reach a wider audience. For example, the Internal Revenue Service posted Tax Tips videos on YouTube in English, Spanish and sign language, and is in the process of promoting a smartphone application called IRS2Go, which will give users a convenient way of checking their federal refund status and obtaining easy-to-understand tax tips. The U.S. Customs and Border Protection continued using YouTube videos, Twitter and Flickr this past year to proactively release information about seizures and other activities related to its mission. Similarly, the Department of Education notified the public of important events and provided information through its blog, electronic newsletters, Twitter, Facebook, and YouTube. These are just a few of the many examples of notable agency accomplishments that are detailed in the agency Chief FOIA Officer Reports for 2012.

I am also pleased to report that this past fiscal year many agencies were able to reduce their FOIA backlogs. Ten of the fifteen cabinet agencies reduced their backlog of pending requests for Fiscal Year 2011. For example, despite receiving over 3,500 more requests this past fiscal year than in Fiscal Year 2010, the Department of Health and Human Services reduced its backlog by 32%. The Department of Defense made a concerted effort this past year to reduce its backlog, with several of its components raising backlog concerns directly with their senior leadership offices. As a result of these efforts, the Defense Logistics Agency, National Geospatial-Intelligence Agency, and Defense Intelligence Agency reduced their backlogs by 69%, 38%, and 29%, respectively, with the agency overall reducing its backlog by 5%. The

Department of State was able to achieve an impressive backlog reduction of 60% by streamlining its process for handling the substantial amount of referrals it receives each year. The Department of Interior was also able to reduce its backlog, achieving a 25% reduction.

Despite these significant backlog reduction efforts by many of the large Departments, overall the government had an increase in the FOIA request backlog this past fiscal year. This increase can be traced to the dramatic increase in the number of FOIA requests received by the Department of Homeland Security, which, in turn, contributed to a much higher request backlog at that agency.

I am particularly pleased to report on the successes achieved by the Department of Justice. This past fiscal year, the Department increased the number of responses to FOIA requests in which records were released in full or in part. Fiscal Year 2011 also marked the second straight year in which the Department maintained a record high 94.5% release rate for requests involving responsive records. Perhaps even more significant, the Department released records in full in response to 79% of requests where records were released. Further, despite three straight years of receiving over 60,000 requests, the Department increased the number of requests processed and reduced our backlog of pending requests by 26%. A parallel reduction in backlog was achieved for pending administrative appeals, with OIP reducing that backlog by a full 41%. The Department also improved the average processing time for both simple and complex FOIA requests. All of these things, both at DOJ and across the government, are concrete examples of improvements made to the administration of the FOIA. There is still work to be done, but we are continuing to make significant, tangible progress in implementing Attorney General Holder's FOIA Guidelines and President Obama's FOIA Memorandum.

My Office carries out the Department's statutory responsibility to encourage compliance with the FOIA. We have been actively engaged from the very start in a variety of initiatives to inform and educate agency personnel on the Administration's commitment to open government and to specifically encourage compliance with both the letter of the law and the spirit of openness that form the foundation for the directives from the President and the Attorney General.

Our engagement started within two days of issuance of the President's FOIA Memorandum, when OIP sent initial guidance to agencies informing them of the significance of the President's Memorandum and advising them to begin applying the presumption of disclosure immediately to all decisions involving the FOIA. OIP issued extensive written guidance which provided agencies with concrete steps to use and approaches to follow in applying the presumption of openness. In the past two years, OIP has provided agencies with additional guidance addressing a range of issues relating to the FOIA. In issuing this guidance, OIP has listened to concerns raised by the FOIA requester community and on multiple occasions has created policy guidance to specifically address those concerns.

I have also reached out to and met individually with the Chief FOIA Officers of those cabinet agencies that receive and process the overwhelming share of FOIA requests. Additionally, as part of the Department's Open Government Plan, I joined the Associate Attorney General, who is the highest-ranking Chief FOIA Officer in the government, in several meetings with all the Chief FOIA Officers of the cabinet agencies to discuss the implementation of the Attorney General's FOIA Guidelines and other open government initiatives. These meetings have become an invaluable opportunity for the Chief FOIA Officers to hear directly from the

Department of Justice as we promote the goals of the President's and the Attorney General's directives and reinforce our joint commitment to openness and transparency.

Since the issuance of the Attorney General's FOIA Guidelines, OIP has also conducted numerous training sessions specifically focused on the President's and Attorney General's transparency initiative. In 2011, OIP conducted forty-seven separate training sessions for agency personnel and also continued to reach out to the public and the requester community. In 2009, OIP began holding roundtable meetings with interested members of the FOIA requester community to engage in a dialogue and share ideas for improving FOIA administration. In response to the interest expressed by agency FOIA professionals in being able to attend the Requester Roundtables, and the enthusiastic response by the requester community to the idea of meeting with those FOIA professionals, shortly after Sunshine Week last March, OIP held the first-ever FOIA Requester-Agency Town Hall meeting. The Town Hall event was a great success, bringing agency FOIA personnel and frequent FOIA requesters together to exchange ideas, share concerns, and engage in a discussion of common issues. OIP plans to make the FOIA Town Hall an annual event and will be convening the next one in the coming months.

Additionally, OIP is leading the effort to maximize the ability of federal agencies to take advantage of technology to streamline the FOIA process and to improve the online availability of information. In 2010, OIP convened two interagency working groups, one on technology and the other on FOIA Best Practices. This past year, OIP reconvened the FOIA Technology Working Group to provide a forum for interested agencies to exchange ideas and experiences in utilizing technology to improve the administration of the FOIA. The Group engaged in discussions about the tools and applications available to assist with FOIA processing, including technology to aid in the search and review of documents, shared platforms that allow for simultaneous review and comment on documents, and electronic capabilities that automatically identify duplicative material.

Leading by example, several of the Department's components, including OIP, have begun utilizing document management software typically used in the litigation context to respond to discovery requests. These components have used this software to more efficiently process large volumes of responsive material. For example, the Bureau of Alcohol, Tobacco, Firearms and Explosives used e-discovery tools to improve its search capabilities and reduce the time needed to review large electronic files. The Civil Rights Division has used software to search and "de-duplicate" large volumes of records. Moreover, the technology used by the Environment and Natural Resources Division allows for simultaneous review and versatility when sorting through voluminous records.

The advantages seen by automating these processes are clearly evident. Conducting an adequate search for responsive records often involves the review of both paper and electronic records originating with multiple Department staff members. In turn, these searches can locate hundreds, if not thousands, of pages of material that need to be reviewed for both responsiveness and duplication before a FOIA disclosure analysis can be conducted. Employing electronic systems that can consolidate and perform some of these necessary administrative tasks allows the Department's FOIA staff to focus their efforts on reviewing responsive material for disclosure. The Department will continue to develop its capabilities in this use of technology with the goal of helping all agencies employ similar tools for the overall benefit of FOIA administration. The Department is currently researching new technologies that will substantially improve the efficiency of the FOIA consultation process by allowing multiple components and agencies to review and comment on material simultaneously.

As you know, each year, agencies submit to the Department of Justice their Annual FOIA Reports, which contain detailed statistics on the number of requests and appeals received and processed, their disposition, and the time taken to respond. This past year, OIP updated both its guidance for preparing the Annual Reports and the tool developed by the Department which assists agencies in providing their data in an "open" format as required by the Open Government Directive. The Department continues to receive very positive feedback from agencies on the value of using the tool, with its built-in math checks and other features that alert agencies to data integrity issues. Agency Annual FOIA Reports for Fiscal Year 2011 are posted together on OIP's website and the data from the reports has been added to FOIA.Gov, the Department's new government-wide, comprehensive FOIA website.

FOIA.Gov has revolutionized the way in which FOIA data is made available to the public. While initially envisioned as a "dashboard" to illustrate statistics collected from agency Annual FOIA Reports, the Department almost immediately began to expand its capabilities and we continue to add new features each year. With well over a million visitors since it was launched last March, the website has become a valuable resource for both the requester community and agency FOIA personnel. The website takes the detailed statistics contained in agency Annual FOIA Reports and displays them graphically. FOIA.Gov allows users to search and sort the data in any way they want, so that comparisons can be made between agencies and over time.

FOIA.Gov also serves as an educational resource for the public by providing useful information about how the FOIA works, where to make requests, and what to expect through the FOIA process. Explanatory videos are embedded into the site and there is a section addressing frequently asked questions as well as a glossary of FOIA terms. FOIA contact information is provided for each agency, including their Chief FOIA Officer and all their FOIA Requester Service Centers and FOIA Public Liaisons. Further, the website spotlights significant FOIA releases and gives the public examples of record sets made available by agencies to the public.

In our most recent improvements to the site, we expanded its scope in yet another way by adding a new feature designed to help the public locate information. We added a search tool to FOIA.Gov that allows the public to enter search terms on any topic of interest. FOIA.Gov then searches for information on that topic across all federal government websites at once. This search tool captures not just those records posted in agency FOIA Libraries, but also records posted anywhere on an agency's website. This more expansive search capability is particularly significant given the steady stream of information that agencies are proactively making available on their websites. FOIA.Gov's search tool provides an easy way for a potential FOIA requester to first easily see what information is already available on a topic. This might preclude the need to even make a request in the first instance, or might allow for a more targeted request to be made.

We launched yet another new feature just a few weeks ago, by including hyperlinks to agency online request forms. As agencies look for ways to improve the FOIA process and increase efficiency, many have developed the capability to accept FOIA requests online. Currently there are 111 offices throughout the government that provide requesters with the ability to make a request in this way. As part of the Department's continuing efforts to improve FOIA.Gov, we have added links to these online forms to the website to make it easier than ever for individuals to find, and make requests electronically. I am very pleased to report that OIP itself has just launched an online capability which allows the public to make requests for the leadership offices of the Department and file an administrative appeal online. OIP's online portal allows the public to establish their own user accounts so that they can track the status of their request or appeal at any time. Requesters will also receive their determinations from OIP via their online accounts, as well as the documents that respond to their requests. As we move forward the Department will look to enhance the OIP Portal to ensure compliance with the President's National Strategy for Trusted Identities in Cyberspace. This policy calls for the development of interoperable digital credentials that reduce the need for users to create multiple account credentials and passwords to access online services. As more and more agencies add this capability to their FOIA programs they will be harnessing the power of technology to improve FOIA processing, in keeping with the President's and Attorney General's focus on better utilization of technology to make information available to the public.

Looking ahead, as OIP completes its review of the agency Annual FOIA Reports submitted in February and the 2012 Chief FOIA Officer Reports that were just completed, we will assess where agencies stand in their ongoing efforts to improve compliance with the FOIA. OIP will continue its outreach on improving transparency and the use of technology to achieve this important goal. As I stated previously, the Department is committed to achieving the new era of open government that the President envisions. We have made significant progress in the past three years toward that goal, but OIP will continue to work diligently to help agencies achieve even greater transparency in the years ahead.

In closing, the Department of Justice looks forward to working with the Subcommittee on all matters pertaining to the government-wide administration of the FOIA, including the use of technology to increase transparency and to improve agencies' administration of the FOIA. I would be pleased to address any question that you or any other Member of the Subcommittee might have on this important subject.

Mr. KELLY. Thank you very much, Ms. Pustay.
Ms. Nisbet.

STATEMENT OF MIRIAM NISBET

Ms. NISBET. Good afternoon, Chairman Kelly and Representative Connolly.

Thank you for the opportunity to appear before you to discuss the Freedom of Information Act and information technology.

I heard from your opening remarks that you both have a sense of some of the challenges that face the government, the 15 Cabinet level departments and the 84 agencies that administer the FOIA. We certainly have seen that.

As you know, the Open Government Act of 2007, which amended the FOIA, created our office to do several things: to review agency policies, procedures and compliance with the law; to recommend policy changes to Congress and the President to improve the administration of FOIA; and also to resolve disputes between FOIA requestors and the Federal agencies.

We opened our doors two and a half years ago in September 2009. Our work has reached customers in 48 States, the District of Columbia and 13 foreign countries. Individuals, including veterans, researchers, professors, journalists, attorneys and inmates comprise more than three-quarters of our workload. Our cases in fiscal year 2011 involved 42 Federal agencies including all 15 Cabinet level departments.

In carrying out our mission, therefore, we do see how agencies are using technology every day to administer FOIA, tracking requests, searching for and reviewing records, posting frequently requested records online, and using agency websites to provide information about FOIA resources.

In 1996, Congress passed the Electronic Freedom of Information Act amendments or the e-FOIA to clarify that the law applies to electronic records as well as traditional paper records. Sixteen years later, agencies are still working to fully implement the e-FOIA. Agencies continue to improve and modernize their processes but improvements can still be made, as you both have noted.

Some obstacles that we have noticed are outdated technology and challenges posed by the need to properly manage electronic records. Certainly my parent agency, the National Archives and Records Administration, takes those needs and concerns to heart and works on those every day.

Mr. Battin, from the Environmental Protection Agency, is going to give you details of the FOIA Module, a one-stop shop portal for FOIA requests. My agency is a partner in that project with EPA and the Department of Commerce because we believe it has great potential to improve the public access to government information and to save taxpayers money by sharing agency resources and adapting existing technology. Other departments and agencies have expressed interest in the partnership and we hope they will join us. The FOIA Module is scheduled to be launched for agencies this summer and unveiled to the public in October.

An area in which FOIA and technology intersect is with proactive disclosure of government records. The e-FOIA amendments require every agency's website to include certain information made public under FOIA. Agencies are continuing to make additional information available on their websites in rather staggering amounts.

In order to ease the public's navigation across agency websites, we are encouraging them to standardize FOIA sites to ensure a customer friendly and efficient way for the public to find FOIA resources. Last week in observance of Sunshine Week, the national initiative to promote open government, OGIS posted on its blog some suggestions to improve the FOIA process administratively such as top-down support for FOIA, developing with stakeholder input, an easy to use template for agencies to customize; standardizing and indexing online FOIA reading rooms; and providing full contact information to designated FOIA professionals.

Finally, OGIS has observed that collaboration across agencies is a cost effective and beneficial tool for exploring ways to improve the administration of FOIA through existing technology. There are several efforts underway in the Federal FOIA community to look for ways to collect the information technology requirements of FOIA professionals and communicate those to companies that create products for them to use to identify technologies that agencies now use that can be repurposed for FOIA; and to share knowledge about FOIA issues such as complex database requests and best practices to help agencies handle them better.

We appreciate the Subcommittee's efforts to examine ways that FOIA can work better and more efficiently for everybody, the public and the agencies. We thank you for the opportunity to testify.

[Prepared statement of Ms. Nisbet follows:]

TESTIMONY OF MIRIAM NISBET

DIRECTOR OF THE OFFICE OF GOVERNMENT INFORMATION SERVICES,

NATIONAL ARCHIVES AND RECORDS ADMINISTRATION

BEFORE THE

HOUSE SUBCOMMITTEE ON TECHNOLOGY, INFORMATION POLICY,

INTERGOVERNMENTAL RELATIONS AND PROCUREMENT REFORM ON

"THE FREEDOM OF INFORMATION ACT AND INFORMATION TECHNOLOGY"

MARCH 21, 2012

Good afternoon, Chairman Lankford, Representative Connolly, and members of the subcommittee. I am Miriam Nisbet, Director of the Office of Government Information Services at the National Archives and Records Administration. Thank you for the opportunity to appear before you to discuss the administration of the Freedom of Information Act (FOIA) and information technology.

I hope to provide you with a sense of some of the challenges facing the 15 Cabinet-level departments and 84 agencies that administer FOIA and how information technology can help make the FOIA process more efficient, effective and transparent for both agencies and requesters. Congress created OGIS as part of the OPEN Government Act of 2007, which amended the FOIA. The Office was created to review agency FOIA policies, procedures and compliance; to recommend policy changes to Congress and the President to improve the administration of FOIA, and to resolve FOIA disputes between agencies and requesters. We opened in September 2009.

More than 1,200 FOIA requesters from nearly every state and points around the globe turned to OGIS for assistance in its first two years. Requests for help ranged from questions about how to file a FOIA request and how to appeal an agency release determination to more difficult inquiries about resolving disputes pertaining to specific exemption use or agency FOIA policy. OGIS opened 764 cases in response to those requests for assistance, 391 in its first year and 373 in its second year, ending September 30, 2011. Between June 2010, when OGIS began tracking phone and e-mail "quick assists," and the end of Fiscal Year (FY) 2011, the Office helped nearly 500 callers and e-mailers. OGIS's work has reached customers from 48 states, the District of Columbia, the Northern Mariana Islands, Puerto Rico and 13 foreign countries, including Australia, Cambodia, Canada, France, India, Iraq and Mexico. Individuals, including veterans, researchers, professors, journalists, attorneys and inmates, comprised more than three-quarters of OGIS's FY 2011 caseload. OGIS cases in FY 2011 involved 42 Federal agencies, including all 15 cabinet-level departments.

OGIS spent FY 2011 preparing for a new website and permanent case management system, launched at the beginning of FY 2012. The new system allows customers to request assistance online and track their OGIS cases while helping OGIS staffers to better manage their caseloads. OGIS's blog, The FOIA Ombudsman: Information and Advice, launched in March 2011 and is designed to stimulate conversation about all things FOIA.

In carrying out our mission, we see how agencies use technology to administer FOIA—tracking requests, searching for and reviewing records, posting frequently requested records online, and using agency websites to provide information about the FOIA process.

In 1996, Congress passed the Electronic Freedom of Information Act Amendments of 1996[1], or e-FOIA, to modernize the then 30-year-old FOIA by clarifying that the law applies to records maintained in electronic format as well as traditional paper records. Specifically, e-FOIA requires agencies to provide records in "any form or format requested if the record is readily reproducible by the agency in that form or format"[2] and to "make reasonable efforts to search for the records in electronic form or format, except when such efforts would significantly interfere with the operation of the agency's automated information system."[3] The law also calls on agencies to expand the role of agency reading rooms by posting more material online, particularly records that have become or are likely to become the subject of subsequent records requests.[4]

Sixteen years later, agencies are still working to fully implement the e-FOIA requirements. While agencies continue to improve and modernize their FOIA processes, OGIS observes that obstacles still remain and improvements can still be made. Some obstacles we have observed are outdated technology and challenges posed by the need to properly manage electronic records. We believe addressing these obstacles will further assist both agencies and requesters to work within the FOIA process.

It was in that landscape that the Environmental Protection Agency (EPA) in 2010 began thinking about ways to address some of those challenges at its agency. One idea was a portal that would automate FOIA processing and reporting. EPA envisioned the eRulemaking

---

[1] Public Law No. 104-231, 110 Stat. 3048

[2] 5 U.S.C. § 552 (a)(3)(B)

[3] 5 U.S.C. § 552 (a)(3)(C)

[4] 5 U.S.C. § 552 (a)(2)(D)

Program's technology infrastructure could be used to accept FOIA requests, store them in a repository for processing by agency staff, and allow responsive documents to be uploaded into the system and posted for the public.

The portal, if successful, would allow requesters to track the status of their requests and find, view and download FOIA requests and agency responses from one site. For its part, the agency could have a secure web site to receive and store requests, assign and process requests, manage records electronically (including referrals to and consultations with other agencies), post responses online, and provide metrics to the Department of Justice for annual reporting.

Rather than build a FOIA portal from the ground up, the EPA envisioned adopting and adapting Regulations.gov, the Federal rulemaking portal launched in 2002, which allows people to comment on Federal regulations and other agency actions. We at OGIS believe strongly that lessons learned through Regulations.gov can be applied efficiently and cost-effectively to FOIA, revolutionizing the FOIA process as Regulations.gov did with rulemaking.

EPA began discussing the pilot portal, now called the FOIA Module, with OGIS and the Department of Commerce in 2010, and formed a partnership in September 2011 (EPA, Commerce and NARA). Other departments and agencies have expressed interest in the partnership and we hope others will join us. For example, the founding partners believe that harmonizing this FOIA Module with the Department of Justice's website FOIA.gov is an idea worth considering.

Representatives from the founding partners met early this year with both agency FOIA professionals and the requester community and will continue those meetings. Comments from both stakeholder groups at the meetings provided the portal's infrastructure team with direction for coding and testing, which is slated for completion later this spring. The FOIA Module is scheduled to be launched for agencies this summer and unveiled to the public in October.

Another area in which FOIA and technology intersect is with proactive disclosure. The E-FOIA Amendments of 1996 require every agency's website to include information made public under FOIA which are likely to be subject to subsequent requests.[5] Agencies are continuing to make additional information available on their websites. In fact, the amount of information is staggering. In order to ease the public's navigation across agencies websites, we are encouraging agencies to standardize FOIA websites to ensure that sites are a customer-friendly and efficient way for the public to find FOIA resources. Last week, in observance of Sunshine Week, a national initiative to promote open government, OGIS posted on its blog suggestions to improve the FOIA process administratively, such as top-down support for FOIA; developing, with stakeholder input, an easy-to-use design template for agencies to customize; standardizing and indexing online FOIA reading rooms; and providing full contact information for designated FOIA professionals.

Finally, OGIS has observed that collaboration is a cost-effective and beneficial tool for exploring ways to improve the administration of FOIA through existing technology. In August 2011, OGIS hosted a meeting of FOIA and IT professionals from the Departments of Defense, Homeland Security, and State, and the Federal Bureau of Investigation to discuss how technology can streamline the FOIA process. Several attendees of that meeting continued the discussion and the FOIA IT Working Group was born in October 2011. This group, one of several in the Executive Branch, is working on ways to

---

[5] 5 U.S.C. § 552 (a)(2)(D).

- collect the IT requirements of FOIA professionals and communicate those to the companies that create products for this audience;

- identify technologies that agencies now use that can be re-purposed for FOIA (such as using the Interlink intranet to streamline consultations and referrals);

- share details about the FOIA Module project; and

- apply the group's unique knowledge to FOIA issues such as database requests and best practices to help agencies better handle such requests.

We share information about the group's efforts with the FOIA community through our blog, The FOIA Ombudsman: Information and Advice, available at: http://blogs.archives.gov/foiablog/.

We are pleased to suggest several improvements to FOIA vis-à-vis information technology and to be a founding partner in the FOIA Module under development by EPA. We believe that the FOIA Module project has the potential to improve FOIA processing, particularly if it is appropriate to adopt broadly. As this project is developed, we believe we will be able to analyze the potential benefits of the system and consider whether the partnership can be expanded.

We appreciate the Subcommittee's efforts to examine ways in which FOIA can work more efficiently for all—agencies and requesters. OGIS stands ready to assist in any way. Thank you for the opportunity to testify; I look forward to answering any questions you may have.

Mr. KELLY. Thank you, Ms. Nisbet.
Mr. Battin.

STATEMENT OF ANDREW BATTIN

Mr. BATTIN. Good afternoon, Chairman Kelly, Representative Connolly and members of the Subcommittee.

My name is Andrew Battin and I am the Director of the Office of Information Collection in the U.S. Environmental Protection Agency's Office of Environmental Information.

I am pleased to appear before you today to discuss the FOIA Module developed in partnership with the Department of Commerce and the National Archives and Records Administration. I am also pleased to join my colleagues from NARA and DOJ on this panel.

EPA is committed to the implementation of the Administration's open government and transparency goals. EPA demonstrated this commitment by striving for reduction in processing time of FOIA requests and recognizing that information technology creates an opportunity to improve our FOIA performance.

EPA has sought continually to be proactive in improving our FOIA administration and to be innovative in the use of technology to enhance our FOIA performance, both internally and for the public. We made it a priority to deploy a system to help track requests and produce EPA's annual FOIA report.

Further, the agency believes that efforts made to improve processing and extend public access to FOIA responsive documents are very much in keeping with the principles of the Administration's open government directive. In embracing the directive mandate for greater transparency, EPA has posted databases from multiple program areas to its website containing information frequently requested under FOIA.

To build on our strong record of transparency, innovative use of available technologies and overall FOIA performance, in June 2010, our Deputy Administrator, Bob Perciasepe, launched a cross-EPA workgroup to identify ways to improve further still the efficiency and consistency of our FOIA processes, to explore the use of tools to inform citizens, as well as to update regulations and policies.

The workgroup report included a recommendation to invest in tools and technologies that streamline FOIA operations and increase public access and transparency. As managing partner of regulations.gov, we explored whether the eRulemaking Program's technology infrastructure could be used to accept FOIA requests.

We procured a third party technical and cost feasibility assessment that concluded that eRulemaking Program's technology infrastructure could be used to accept FOIA requests, store them in a repository for processing by agency staff and allow responsive documents to be uploaded into the system and posted for public access.

These analyses indicated that leveraging the eRulemaking technology infrastructure could be accomplished with a fairly modest investment. EPA shared the analyses with the Federal Government's two FOIA leads, the Department of Justice and the National Archives Administration, to validate the approach of developing a FOIA module.

The module would automate FOIA processing and reporting, store FOIA requests and responses in an electronic records repository and enable the public to search, access and download previously released FOIA responses for participating agencies. The module would also accumulate statistics on FOIA actions throughout the year and summarize this information for an agency's annual FOIA report.

Later, other agencies were invited to learn about and explore the use of a possible FOIA Module. Through this broader outreach, requirements were developed and refined for how such a FOIA Module could operate. We continued our conversations with our Federal partners. Based on the assessment, and a number of agencies expressed interest in the FOIA Module.

Following finalization of the workgroup's recommendation for a FOIA Module, EPA entered a partnership with NARA and the Department of Commerce. These agencies provided funding to help design and develop such a solution. The construction and deployment of the system is estimated to cost $1.3 million. The module is scheduled for partner agencies to use later this summer and available for public submissions by October 2012.

As development of the FOIA Module recently reached a sufficient state of definition to clarify how its component capabilities are expected to work, managers in both EPA and DOJ recognized that it has become timely to harmonize EPA's efforts on the FOIA module with the functions provides by DOJ's FOIA.gov now and in the future.

Accordingly, we have begun a series of conversations about each organization's electronic tools to understand in greater detail any near term, technical coordination needs and to identify potential future complementary capabilities. We look forward to continuing productive, interagency collaboration moving forward on this important work.

I appreciate the opportunity to provide this testimony and would be happy to respond to any questions.

[Prepared statement of Mr. Battin follows:]

TESTIMONY OF
ANDREW BATTIN, DIRECTOR
OFFICE OF INFORMATION COLLECTION
OFFICE OF ENVIRONMENTAL INFORMATION
U.S. ENVIRONMENTAL PROTECTION AGENCY

BEFORE THE

SUBCOMMITTEE ON TECHNOLOGY, INFORMATION POLICY,
INTERGOVERNMENTAL RELATIONS AND PROCUREMENT REFORM
COMMITTEE ON OVERSIGHT AND GOVERNMENT REFORM
U.S. HOUSE OF REPRESENTATIVES

March 21, 2012

Good afternoon Chairman Lankford, Representative Connolly, and members of the

Subcommittee. My name is Andrew Battin, Director of the Office of Information Collection in

the U.S. Environmental Protection Agency's (EPA) Office of Environmental Information. I am

pleased to appear before you today to discuss the development of the FOIA Module being

developed by EPA in partnership with the National Archives and Records Administration and

the Department of Commerce.

EPA is committed to the implementation of the Administration's Open Government and

Transparency goals. EPA demonstrated this commitment by striving for reduction in processing

time of initial Freedom of Information Act (FOIA) requests and recognizing that information

technology creates an opportunity to improve our FOIA performance.

EPA has sought continually to be proactive in improving our FOIA administration and innovative in the use of technology to enhance the FOIA process, both internally and for the public. We made it a priority to deploy a system to help track requests and produce EPA's annual FOIA Report.

Further, the Agency believes that efforts made to improve processing and extend public access to documents that are responsive to FOIA requests is very much in keeping with the letter and spirit of the principles in the Administration's Open Government Directive. Embracing the Directive's mandate for greater transparency, EPA has posted databases from multiple program areas to its website containing information frequently requested under FOIA.

We believe EPA's FOIA performance documents our commitment to openness and continuous improvement. EPA's program and regional offices analyze and respond to more than 10,000 FOIA requests each year. Over the past several years, EPA aggressively tackled its backlog of overdue requests while responding to new requests in a timely manner. In 2001, there were 23,514 overdue FOIA requests, which was 165% of the number of requests received each year by EPA. The Agency revised its FOIA procedures and processes to reduce overdue requests to less than 10% of the number of new requests received each year. By fiscal year 2007, we met our goal and continued to reduce our backlog so that by the end of fiscal year 2011, the Agency's backlog totaled only 226. Furthermore, to ensure consistency in the application of statutory criteria, we moved all fee waivers and expedited processing decisions from the regions to our national office in 2009.

While these improvements and efficiencies have been made, there is still much more

that could be improved by having all publicly released documents made available online as they

become cleared for release in response to a FOIA request. Continued access to these

documents has many benefits. Especially significant here is the capability that better tools can

give us to recapture the effort required to identify, review and prepare a set of documents for

public release. Through a data repository, we could quickly locate that documents if needed

again and minimize the effort to provide the same documents consistently.

To build on our strong record of transparency, innovative use of available technologies,

and overall FOIA performance, in June 2010 our Deputy Administrator, Bob Perciasepe,

launched a cross-EPA workgroup to identify ways to further improve the efficiency and

consistency of our FOIA responses as well as update regulations and policies. His mandate to

the workgroup included better use of tools "to inform citizens in a timely way about what is

known and done by their government...[, and to] recommend[]... any needed changes to ensure

the effective use of such tools." The workgroup report included a recommendation to "invest

in tools and technologies that streamline FOIA operations and increase public access and

transparency."

As managing partner of the eRulemaking Program, EPA noted that the FOIA process

mirrors many of the processes used by the public to review proposed rulemakings and submit

comments into www.regulations.gov. To this end, we explored whether the eRulemaking

Program's technology infrastructure could be used to accept FOIA requests, store them in a repository for processing by agency staff, and allow responsive documents to be uploaded into the system and posted for public access. These analyses indicated that the eRulemaking infrastructure could be used to support FOIA processing. Further, these analyses indicated that leveraging the eRulemaking technology infrastructure could be accomplished with a fairly modest investment.

EPA shared the analyses with the federal government's FOIA leads, the Office of Information Policy at the Department of Justice and the Office of Government Information Services at the National Archives and Records Administration (NARA) to validate the approach of developing a FOIA Module that would improve the processing of FOIA requests operationally at the Agency-level, as well as provide statistics for the Annual FOIA Report. The module would automate FOIA processing and reporting, storing FOIA requests and responses in an electronic records repository, and enable the public to search, access, and download previously released FOIA responses from any participating agency. The module would also accumulate statistics of the operations throughout the year and summarize this for the Annual FOIA Report. Later, other agencies were invited to learn about and explore use of a possible FOIA module. Through this broader outreach, requirements were developed and refined for how such a FOIA module could operate.

EPA went on to procure a third-party technical and cost feasibility assessment. The assessment concluded that the FOIA module could be developed and deployed using the eRulemaking Program's technology infrastructure. Following the finalization of the

workgroup's recommendation for a FOIA module, EPA entered into a partnership with NARA

and the Department of Commerce. These agencies provided funding to help reimburse EPA for

costs to design and develop such a solution. The construction and deployment of the system

for the three Agencies is estimated to cost $1.3 million. The module is scheduled to be

available for partner agencies to use agency use later this summer and available for public

submissions by October 2012.

As development of the FOIA module recently reached a sufficient state of definition to

clarify how its component capabilities are expected to work, managers in both EPA and DOJ

recognized that it has become timely to harmonize EPA's efforts on the FOIA module with the

functions provided by DOJ's FOIA.Gov , now and in the future. Accordingly, we have begun a

series of conversations about each organization's electronic tools to understand in greater

detail any near-term technical coordination needs, and identify potential future complementary

capabilities. We look forward to continuing, productive interagency collaboration moving

forward on this important work.

I appreciate the opportunity to provide this testimony and will be happy to respond to

any questions you may have.

Mr. KELLY. Thank you all. You complete written testimony will be entered in the permanent record.

You were all within the five minutes. That was very good and usually doesn't happen here.

I recognize myself for the first questions.

Ms. Pustay, DOJ says it is going to develop its own portal. Why doesn't it just choose to work with the EPA on theirs?

Ms. PUSTAY. We actually just launched our portal, so we are done with the portal we have. As I mentioned in my testimony, there are 100 agencies that have online request portals, so this has been a wave of use of technology across the government. As I mentioned, one of the focuses of the Attorney General's FOIA guidelines was to encourage agencies to utilize technology, so we have had a whole range of options being explored across the government. Now, as I said, there are up to over 100 agencies with online request portals.

As I mentioned, as a new feature for FOIA.gov is we are including on that website hyperlinks to all the online request forms available across the government to make it easy to reach them through FOIA.gov.

Mr. KELLY. DOJ is responsible for setting FOIA policy and compliance across the government, as well as litigating on behalf of all FOIA lawsuits. Has there ever been a case where the Department of Justice has disagreed with an agency withholding information and refused to defend it?

Ms. PUSTAY. There have definitely been cases where additional information was released as a result of application of the Attorney General's Guidelines. We saw that most especially in the immediate wake of issuance of the Guidelines. That has been three years ago, so we have been working very hard to train agencies, implement and focus on the new requirements to apply foreseeable harm standards, to not withhold information just because you legally can, some of the things we saw the President mention in the video that you showed a moment ago.

At this point, we have a nice engrained understanding of the provisions of the Attorney General's Guidelines across the government.

Mr. KELLY. Last year, a DOJ lawyer told the Supreme Court that "The DOJ does not embrace the principle of openness." Can you explain that disconnect between the President's memo and the DOJ's actions?

Ms. PUSTAY. I am happy you asked me that so I could clear that up.

As I understand it, the exchange that occurred during the course of the Supreme Court argument was simply not that there was a disagreement with the presumption of openness, the actual question being asked of the attorney was whether FOIA exemptions should be interpreted narrowly.

Of course they should be. We have Supreme Court precedence that says FOIA exemptions should be interpreted narrowly, but there is a corollary principle and that is that FOIA exemptions must also be given meaningful reach and application consistent with the fact that Congress included in the FOIA exemptions for a purpose, to protect vital interests like personal privacy and national security.

He was attempting to explain that the concept of narrow inter-
pretation of exemptions had to be analyzed in reference to the corollary principle, that exemptions must also be given meaningful
reach.

Mr. KELLY. Thank you.

The purpose of the hearing is to examine ways to use technology
to improve transparency. What do you think are the most important advances in this area? What are the biggest challenges? Each of
you has very unique perspectives on this. Mr. Battin, why don't you
start? We will give Ms. Pustay a chance to catch her breath. Mr.

BATTIN. I certainly think the biggest challenge we face, and one of
the main reasons we went into development of the Module, was to
improve our efficiencies in being able to meet the public de- mand.

Through the use of the Module, we are internally focusing on
improving the process to answer FOIAs, bring consistency to the
process and create a repository for future use.

For the public, we are increasing transparency, allowing them to
submit online, track their progress throughout and have access in
the end. All these are challenges that we face through some of our
antiquated approaches.

Mr. KELLY. Ms. Nisbet?

Ms. NISBET. Representative Kelly, I think that the partnership
that you heard about and the effort to build a one-stop shop portal
really gives you an indication of where a lot of people think the future of technology is going to take us with having something that
is really easy for the public so they don't have to go to 350 places
to make a request, to be able to quickly see what information has
been already disclosed and is publicly available so maybe they don't
even have to make a request.

On the other side is to make easier for agencies to share the resources they have and also to process requests in a more efficient
way. We have many different systems out there and trying to find
ways we can actually share with each what we already have with
each other instead of coming up with so many different solutions
I think this has some natural cost avoidance built in.

Mr. KELLY. Thank you.

Ms. Pustay?

Ms. PUSTAY. I will mention something we haven't talked about
yet so far this afternoon.

One important thing is as agencies have been working very diligently to proactively post information, to anticipate interest in
records and put those records, sometimes more than records, put
databases, put whole websites up dedicated to particular topics,
they are really working to try to anticipate interest in records and
get information out to the public before a request is even made.

There are lots of releases being made by agencies separate and
apart from FOIA. That is great because that is part of the Attorney
General's Guidelines as well.

One thing we think is important is to have the ability to capture
all that information. That was one of the reasons we put on
FOIA.gov the find tab so that if you are a researcher or a student,
and you're looking for information on a particular topic, there is a
way to look across agency websites and capture them.

Going to the next level, what we are working on now at the Department is metadata tagging. Our plan is to work with GSA to actually have standardized ways to tag records before they are posted, to make the search process for them even that much more precise. We have to be careful as agencies are very enthusiastically putting information up on the web. Websites can easily become overwhelmed with data. It is very important that there be a way to find the information you are looking for.

Mr. KELLY. Thank you.

I will now recognize the Ranking Member, Mr. Connolly.

Mr. CONNOLLY. Thank you, Mr. Chairman, and welcome to our panelists.

I spent 14 years in local government before coming here and in the Commonwealth of Virginia, we actually have some of the most stringent FOIA laws in the United States. By the way, the FOIA laws do not apply to the State Legislature, of course.

My schedule was subject to FOIA, my phone lines was subject to FOIA, my emails were subject to FOIA. I had to deal with FOIA requests personally and as chairman on behalf of the county government and sometimes they would be overly broad requests that were not very specific. It was very hard to respond to them without producing reams of material that presumably the requestor didn't really intend.

A lot of times if the FOIA came from the press and were overly broad to try to make sure they didn't draw it so narrowly that we only juridically answered the exact question they made. They tried to often make them overly broad and we would have to negotiate with them and say you need to be more specific, otherwise you will get the Encyclopedia Britannica printed.

I have seen the challenges of FOIA. All good attorneys, and certainly our county attorney, always advised agencies and individuals in the local government, whatever you do, do not stall, do not stonewall, don't try to create barriers to responding in a timely fashion or you can find yourself prosecuted, you can find yourself in violation of the law.

With that introduction, Ms. Pustay, maybe I can start with you, presumably there is also similar guidance given to Federal agencies in terms of by and large you have to assume it is a legitimate request and be responsive. Would that be fair?

Ms. PUSTAY. Absolutely. There is a whole range of things that agencies do routinely and certainly as part of our outreach and training to agencies, my office conducts training throughout the year. Every year, we reach thousands of agency employees. There are many different techniques actually to use when working with requestors.

The big advantage of open communication with requestors about what they are looking for is that if the requestor can be more precise, the information can be provided to them more promptly. Requestors understand that and are always very happy to work with agencies. Maybe not always very happy, but usually very happy to work with agencies to help focus their request.

Mr. CONNOLLY. Right.

Ms. PUSTAY. Also, there is a real push right now across the government to increase efficiency again as part of the AG's Guidelines specifically directed toward looking for more efficient ways to respond to requests. We are seeing that agencies are processing more requests. They processed 30,000 more last year, releasing more information.

There is a bigger picture here where agencies overall are looking to be cooperative to implement the FOIA guidelines.

Mr. CONNOLLY. If I could ask, maybe Ms. Nisbet wants to chime in here too, the Chairman alluded to some barrier, some problem still going on, the cost of providing material sometimes seemingly exorbitant and delays. So, those are two metrics I wonder are we measuring that we are bringing down the response time so that we are more responsive? Are we also measuring the other impediments that the Chairman rightfully cited such as the cost of providing the material requested so that we are not needlessly creating barriers for people?

Ms. NISBET. I think trying to deal with those kinds of early speed bumps is something I know my office has worked very hard on. As you know, part of our mission is resolving disputes between FOIA requestors and the agency. We deal with those every day. Fees and delays continue to be some of our largest numbers of cases.

They are still a problem but also we see a corresponding emphasis on customer service, on picking up that phone as quickly as you can and talking to the requestor to be able to talk about the scope of the request so that you don't have lots of time spent looking for something the requestor is not even interested in. Those are very, very fundamental customer service things that we certainly are seeing people trying to do a better job of.

Mr. CONNOLLY. Mr. Chairman, I see my time is up. How does the Chair wish to proceed? I do have a few more questions.

Mr. KELLY. We will do another round.

Mr. CONNOLLY. All right. I yield to the Chair.

Mr. KELLY. The Open Government Act changes fee waivers and statuses and I know there is some confusion out there. We played the President's remarks and maybe created a Pandora's Box but didn't mean to. When we start telling people about openness, transparency and everybody will have access to almost everything and anything you want and anytime you want it, I understand.

I am not a lifetime politician. In fact, I have only been here a year or so. I understand you can say things that sometimes sound good in front of a group and you turn back to the agencies that handle them and say, my God, I wish I hadn't said that, it creates a lot of problems for us, but there are a lot of lawsuits, are there not? Why do we have so much trouble with the excessive fees? Ms. Nisbet, maybe you can weigh in on that. I know the Ranking Member asked something about that but there is some concern out there.

Ms. NISBET. Representative Kelly, there is a lot of confusion both amongst requestors and agencies about how the fee categories work and the fee waivers. I think this is one of the first things a FOIA public liaison officer, a FOIA customer service center can do, is to work with the requestors to explain them.

As I mentioned, my office has a number of cases that revolve around fees. That can definitely be a barrier but if you walk

through what the requirements are both for the fee category you
are in as well as the fee waivers, it can really help.

I will give you an example. Last year, we had a requestor come
to us concerned because it had gotten a bill for $450,000 to process
a big database request. Working with the agency, which was very
cooperative, and the requestor who was seeking to avoid the lawsuit, to resolve those issues pretty quickly and get to the substance
of the case.

Mr. KELLY. Ms. Pustay, in your opening statement, you said 93.1
percent of requests were handled. There is some confusion on that.
The White House claims 93 percent but they didn't include cases
that were no response of record, cases where the request was considered by the agency to be improper, or cases where the requestor
did not pay fees for records. When all those cases are included, the
response rate drops down to only a 65 percent rate and a lot of
those are heavily redacted.

When we talk about response rate, the American public often-
times feels we are being gamed, they are being told one thing and
the actual figures seem to go in a different direction. Maybe you
could clear up that for us?

Ms. PUSTAY. Sure. I am happy to and I am glad you asked that
question.

We refer to it as a release rate actually. First, in terms of the
overall numbers, to address your last point, all the detailed statistics about the numbers of requests that are handled by an agency,
the disposition of the request, to get to your comment about how
much time it takes, all of that is incredibly detailed information
and is all required to be prepared very year by every single agency
as part of their annual FOIA report. All this information is publicly
available.

We then take all that information and have it on FOIA.gov now
where it is easily manipulated, compared and contracted. In terms
of accountability and transparency about how agencies are doing,
the annual FOIA reports and FOIA.gov's graphic representation of
that data is what should give you confidence that you are seeing
the statistics however you want them.

To get to your question about a release rate and how we calculate it, the reason we calculate it by not every single request that
is processed, we calculate a release rate based on those requests
where there are records to be processed because it is only for those
requests that the agency has the decision to make, do I release or
do I withhold.

Out of those requests, where an agency is actually looking at the
record and deciding, do I release or withhold, in 93 percent of those
requests information is released either in full or in part.

Mr. KELLY. So the 65 percent we talk about is an actual rate. Is
that more accurate than the 93 percent?

Ms. PUSTAY. Respectfully, it doesn't make sense to calculate a release rate based on the requests where there were no records, for
example. Where there are no records, the agency never has a
chance to say I want to release or I am going to withhold because
there physically are no records in response to that request. To have
the release rate be meaningful, it is based on those requests where
there are records.

Mr. KELLY. When we respond to people, we are setting the parameters saying this is what we could do based on what we did have and what we came away with?

Ms. PUSTAY. Exactly.

Mr. KELLY. So there is a clarification on that. That is how you come up with the 93 percent.

Ms. PUSTAY. We say the release rate is based on looking at the numbers of requests where records were processed for disclosure. That is the reason why I say processed for disclosure.

Mr. KELLY. Okay. That is the key, processed for disclosure?

Ms. PUSTAY. Yes.

Mr. KELLY. Not on number of requests?

Ms. PUSTAY. Exactly.

Mr. KELLY. Mr. Connolly?

Mr. CONNOLLY. Thank you, Mr. Chairman.

Ms. Pustay, picking up on something the Chairman was referring to, why would we ever redact something in a FOIA response?

Ms. PUSTAY. Of course, there are nine exemptions that Congress put into the statute to provide protection for a range of information. Personal privacy is the most frequently used reason to protect information.

Mr. CONNOLLY. First of all, Congress provided for that?

Ms. PUSTAY. That is right.

Mr. CONNOLLY. Secondly, that requires someone to actually go over the documents to make sure we are appropriately redacting pursuant to these nine exemptions?

Ms. PUSTAY. Exactly.

Mr. CONNOLLY. That takes a little time which could add to the backlog not because anyone is trying to prevent information from getting into public hands but because actually we are trying to protect the innocent and sensitive material?

Ms. PUSTAY. Of course.

Mr. CONNOLLY. Let me ask a different question of you, Ms. Nisbet, because your office is sort of the ombudsman for the Federal Government.

Surely there is a difference between a FOIA request at EPA, for example, I want to see the studies on lead in water, I want to see the empirical evidence that led you to decide to regulate that issue, no national secrets there versus a FOIA request that says I want to see the Department of Homeland Security's assessment of strategic assets and the plans to protect them, how many are vulnerable and how many are secure, I would like to see that, please. Fair enough? There is a difference?

We have to manage those two requests even though they are both FOIA requests with different levels of sensitivity, awareness and scrutiny. Would that be fair?

Ms. NISBET. That is correct, sir.

Mr. CONNOLLY. Just using those two examples, in terms of the time, resources, backlog, responsiveness, protecting national assets, maybe I am a terrorist making that request using the Freedom of Information Act because I want to save myself research time, I want you to do it. How do we protect ourselves and how do we differentiate in these requests as a Federal Government between one and the other?

Ms. NISBET. That is why you have very dedicated FOIA professionals who work on these kinds of issues every day.

The processing of requests, as you point out, can be fairly simple
particularly when there is an easy search in one place and the response is, we don't have any records, to agencies or departments
that are quite decentralized and a search would require, for example, with the State Department, not only looking in Washington
but looking overseas.

As well and checking for whether or not there were responsive
records, gathering those records, determining whether there they
are really responsive, reviewing them and particularly if they deal
with classified information or with sensitive information whether it
is financial, personal privacy, whatever the nature of the records,
or maybe all of those in one document, reviewing them carefully to
be sure a release to one is a release to all and that a release to
one person who might be a very legitimate researcher is not going
to also be turned into something harmful by a requestor who
doesn't have a beneficial idea.

Mr. CONNOLLY. In other words, we have to sometimes exercise
some prudent judgment?

Ms. NISBET. Every day.

Mr. CONNOLLY. When we do that, it is always, in a sense, an arbitrary line. We are drawing a line saying no, we are not going to
go on that there side. It is a matter of opinion whether that is the
appropriate line or it should be moved out here or whether there
should be any at all. Nonetheless, the people making that judgment
have to make that judgment?

Ms. NISBET. And they have to make a decision so that the requestor can know what are you going to get, are you going to get
anything, how many pages or are you not going to get anything,
and also that they get an answer.

Mr. CONNOLLY. Right. A lot of our economic competitors in the
world don't have FOIA. You can't go to Beijing and FOIA their
plans for X, Y, Z, or Tehran or lots of other places.

Mr. Chairman, would you indulge me just to ask Mr. Battin if
he could take a little bit of time to talk us through how their portal
works and why so many people see it as perhaps a model for other
Federal agencies. By the way, where are you from?

Mr. BATTIN. I thank you for both questions, Congressman. I am
from Pennsylvania. I grew up in Pennsylvania.

In terms of how the Module works, the Module is designed to
provide a single place for the three participating agencies to allow
the public to come in and submit a request, to track that request
in a very open and transparent way so they know within the 20-
day period that we are looking to respond where in the process
their request is.

Also it is designed to give them an opportunity to have a dialogue if there are issues that need to be clarified with the FOIA
staff and the requestor. There is now a forum to do that.

Next is providing access to the public to receive those answers
so they can go to a particular spot, not only look at their request
and answers to that request but other questions that may have
been asked. That is kind of the public side of this.

On the inside internal to the benefits to the agencies, a lot of what we are stressing is processing efficiencies, the consistency in responses, having that repository for reuse so that we don't have to begin answering questions from the beginning again. Our current solutions don't have that repository that we can go back to and answer a question day forward. That is a huge resource drain when we have to recreate the answers time and again.

Also providing referrals to other agencies as is necessary, within the system we have the ability to refer to our partnering agencies if there is a question or maybe it should be directed to them and providing that ability to enable a repository for searching for other agency purposes such as electronic discovery. That is something Ms. Pustay mentioned in the beginning. Having that repository of electronically discovered information preassembled is very important.

Mr. CONNOLLY. Thank you.

Mr. Chairman, thank you for your indulgence.

Mr. KELLY. Thank you, sir. It is nice working with you. It is easy.

That is going to end the questioning for the first panel. We appreciate your being here today.

I think we would both agree, I have only been with Mr. Connolly for a year, the service you provide our country is very great. Sometimes you have to appear before a committee and it seems maybe we are at you for a certain reason, but we do represent the people of the United States and we think it is very important that there is a clear and transparent approach to everything we do in this government.

Thank you so much for being here today. We appreciate your indulgence.

We are going to take a short recess and then we will have the second panel.

Mr. CONNOLLY. I thank you for your sentiments, Mr. Chairman.

[Recess.]

Mr. KELLY. We will now welcome our second panel. Mr. Sean Moulton is the Director of Federal Information Policy at OMB Watch. Mr. Moulton, thank you for being here with us today.

Pursuant to Committee rules, all witnesses must be sworn before they testify. Please rise and raise your right hand.

Do you solemnly swear or affirm that the testimony you are about to give will be the truth, the whole truth, and nothing but the truth?

[Witness responds in the affirmative.]

Mr. KELLY. May the record reflect that the witness answered in the affirmative.

In order to allow time for discussion, if you could, please stay within the five minutes. As you have seen, we are pretty liberal with that. I am not usually liberal that way but sometimes I am. Being beside Mr. Connolly, I am being a little more liberal today.

We are going to allow you your opening statement somewhere in the five minute range, please.

STATEMENT OF SEAN MOULTON, DIRECTOR, FEDERAL INFORMATION POLICY, OMB WATCH

Mr. MOULTON. Chairman Kelly, Ranking Member Connolly, members of the Subcommittee, thank you for inviting me to testify today on the important topic of how technology can improve implementation of the Freedom of Information Act.

My name is Sean Moulton. I am the Director of Federal Information Policy at OMB Watch, an independent, non-partisan organization that advocates for more open, accountable government.

Improving citizen access to public information has been an important part of our work for 30 years. We also have experience using technology to make government information more available to the public online.

I will begin with a look at the current situation of FOIA implementation. Last week, OMB Watch published our assessment of FOIA performance at 25 agencies. Our assessment evaluated processing of FOIA requests, the rates of requests granted and the use of exemptions. Across these issues, the news is mixed, with progress in some areas as well as a few setbacks.

In 2011, the Obama Administration increased its FOIA processing and processed the highest number of requests since 2005. Unfortunately, the number of requests received increased even faster, resulting in a rise in the overall backlog. Although many agencies have made progress in reducing their backlogs, continued improvement is still needed.

In terms of granting requests, 2011 added to the Obama Administration's three-year average of a 95 percent granting request rate whether in full or in part. This is higher than the Bush Administration's average of 93 percent or the last years of the Clinton Administration at 89 percent. However, the Obama Administration more often partially granted requests compared to the previous Administrations.

Finally, on exemptions, the total use of exemptions dropped by 7 percent. Notably, the use of the most discretionary exemption declined as well in 2011. Use of Exemption 2, internal agency rules, decreased by 63 percent. Use of Exemption 5, for interagency memoranda, fell by 14 percent. These declines come after steady growth in the use of both exemptions during the Bush Administration.

Turning now to the issue of technology, OMB Watch strongly believes that technology can improve FOIA performance. For several years, OMB Watch has advocated for the development of a robust electronic FOIA system that incorporates three main improvements: allowing the public to submit and track requests electronically at a centralized site; improved communication through the use of email; and to post online in a searchable system documents released through FOIA.

Many of these needed reforms are embodied in the FOIA portal project being led by EPA. The project will provide a single interface for the public to submit requests to any participating agency and would modernize the infrastructure agencies used for processing, tracking requests and publishing information. When completed, we believe the FOIA portal will help agencies process requests faster at a lower cost while expanding online disclosures and improving requestors' experience.

Mail delays and postage costs would be reduced through online communications. The portal would also speed up consultations and referrals between agencies. Released documents would be uploaded to a public website available both to the requestor as well as to any other searchers. Withheld documents would remain in the system restricted from public access but quickly available to agency review in the event of an appeal.

Although the project is at an early stage, we believe it merits support from Congress. Congress should make it clear that it expects every agency to participate in such a centralized e-FOIA system. Congress can also play a helpful oversight role to ensure that such a system maintains high standards of usability for the public. In addition to the FOIA portal, OMB Watch recommends other key technology reforms to improve FOIA. These suggested reforms include: update the electronic FOIA provisions to strengthen the standard for publishing released FOIA documents online; expand the types of information agencies are required to proactively post on their websites; establish a government-wide, online document disclosure goal; and update the e-Government Act to better address electronic records management and disclosure needs in IT procurement decisions.

In conclusion, OMB Watch is fully committed to the Committee's goals of using modern technology to improve transparency. With the right reforms and investments, FOIA can be quicker, easier to use and more proactive in disclosing information to the public.

I sincerely thank you for the opportunity to address this Committee and I look forward to your questions.

[Prepared statement of Mr. Moulton follows:]

Testimony of Sean Moulton
Director of Federal Information Policy
OMB Watch

Before the
U.S. House of Representatives
Committee on Oversight and Government Reform
Subcommittee on Technology, Information Policy, Intergovernmental Relations and
Procurement Reform

On
FOIA in the 21st Century: Using Technology to Improve Transparency in Government

March 21, 2012

Chairman Lankford, Ranking Member Connolly, members of the subcommittee: My name is Sean Moulton and I am the Director of Federal Information Policy at OMB Watch -- an independent, nonpartisan organization that advocates for more open, accountable government. Improving citizen access to public information has been an important part of our work for almost 30 years. Mr. Chairman, Mr. Connolly, thank you for your continuing interest and commitment to this issue, and thank you for inviting me to testify today on the important topic of how technology can improve implementation of the Freedom of Information Act (FOIA).

OMB Watch has long advocated for better implementation of the Freedom of Information Act – for greater online disclosure on agency websites, for enforcement mechanisms if agencies fail to honor FOIA requests, and for robust congressional oversight. We also have experience using technology to help make public information more accessible. In 1989, before widespread public and commercial use of the Internet, we began operating the Right-To-Know Network (RTK NET), an electronic service providing public access to data collected by the Environmental Protection Agency. In recent years, we played a leadership role in encouraging the policies incorporated in the Federal Funding Accountability and Transparency Act of 2006 (FFATA), which mandated that federal spending data be displayed on a website, with searchable and downloadable data. In 2006, we developed FedSpending.org, a website that implemented so many of the legislation's goals, that it was licensed to the federal government and became the starting point for USAspending.gov, which was launched at the end of 2007.

We believe that in a democracy, citizens should have easy access to the information that their government gathers – all but the most sensitive information. Without information, citizens cannot engage with their representatives and their public officials as equal partners. This was the logic behind the passage of FOIA in 1966 and remains the driving force for transparency. But too often, requesting government information is a confusing, slow, and frustrating process. We believe technology can and should streamline and speed up citizen requests for public information and expand proactive disclosure.

1. The Goals of FOIA Implementation

OMB Watch has long been advocating for more investments in FOIA technology and improved processing systems. The passage of the Electronic FOIA Amendments in 1996[1] was a major step in laying out that technology should be used to improve the FOIA process. While the last three administrations tried to implement these requirements, the open government community has been disappointed by the results.

In 2007-2008, OMB Watch convened more than 100 leaders and experts from the open government community and developed numerous recommendations on how to improve government openness. Several recommendations focused on using technology to improve FOIA processing. Our recommendations today build on and expand those recommendations.

We recommend the development of a robust E-FOIA system that would allow the public to submit and track requests at a centralized site and to receive responses electronically. Such a system would:

- Allow the public to submit electronic requests either by e-mail or through an agency website (This would require posting an e-mail address on each agency website and in each agency's FOIA regulations, as well as establishing a web form for FOIA requests);
- Include an easy-to-understand explanation of how to submit a FOIA request, how the agency will process the request, and the individual's rights and responsibilities under the agency's FOIA procedures (Agencies should also include links to more detailed information, such as the agency's FOIA regulations, the Office of Government Information Services (OGIS) website, and FOIA.gov);
- Ensure that FOIA requesters can communicate easily with the agency by widely publicizing the contact information, including telephone and e-mail address, of the FOIA office;
- Establish an online service to allow FOIA requesters to automatically check the status of their request or appeal by entering the tracking number on a website;
- Establish categories of the records that can be proactively posted online regularly; and
- Post online, in a searchable system, all significant documents released under any FOIA request – without waiting for a second FOIA request.

2. Progress in Improving FOIA Implementation

Over the years, there have many efforts to improve the functioning of FOIA. For instance:

- President George W. Bush issued Executive Order 13392 in December 2005 to help improve the processing of FOIA requests. The order required agencies to conduct internal assessments of FOIA service problems and develop workplans to make

---

[1] P.L. 104-231.

improvements. It established new positions within the agencies, such as FOIA Request Service Centers and Public Liaison officials, to work with requestors. The order seemed to deliver some results: the number of requests awaiting processing reached its peak in 2006. Backlogs then shrank each year in 2007, 2008, and 2009.

- The OPEN Government Act of 2007[2] required agencies to create a FOIA tracking system that allows requestors to monitor the progress of requests on the Internet or by telephone. In addition, the law created the Office of Government Information Services (OGIS) within the National Archives and Records Administration to serve as an ombudsman for the FOIA system. The law also penalizes agencies that fail to respond to FOIA requests within the required 20 days by barring them from collecting search and duplication fees. Moreover, the law required agencies to clearly state the amount of information deleted in its redactions and the exemption invoked for making each individual redaction.
- The OPEN FOIA Act of 2009[3] increased the transparency of proposed new exemptions to FOIA.

We were pleased that President Obama's January 2009 FOIA memo, the attorney general's March 2009 FOIA memo, and the Open Government Directive of December 2009 all instructed agencies to proactively disseminate information online to reduce the necessity of filing FOIA requests.

Some agencies' Open Government Plans, which were required under the Open Government Directive, included developing, improving, or maintaining the agency's FOIA tracking system. However, progress across executive agencies in implementing these plans has been lurching and uneven.

In Nov. 2010 OGIS issued a best FOIA practices document[4] that is periodically updated. The list of practices include recommendations that agencies "develop an online or e-mail system for filing FOIA requests" and "establish [an] online procedure for tracking appeal status." Some agencies have made progress in establishing such systems. For example, the Treasury Department launched an online request form in April 2011. However, few have any online tracking system in place.

In addition, OGIS specifically encourages agencies to "post online significant documents that have been released under FOIA without waiting for a second FOIA request." Some agencies frequently post requested documents online. For instance, the Department of Energy posted all of its responses to FOIA requests from January to May 2009. Other agencies reported using past FOIA requests as the means to identify their high-value datasets to be posted on Data.gov. In addition, the Federal Communications Commission's National Broadband Plan, released in March 2010, recommended that agencies post online all responses to FOIA requests.

There are also some agencies that post logs of FOIA requests. For instance, predating the Obama administration, some parts of the Department of Defense (DOD) have posted their FOIA logs on an annual basis. DOD has subsequently added these FOIA logs as datasets on Data.gov. The

---

[2] P.L. 110-175.
[3] P.L. 111-83, Sec. 564.
[4] https://ogis.archives.gov/Assets/Best+Practices+Chart+Agencies.pdf.

Department of Homeland Security began posting its FOIA logs on a monthly basis during the Obama administration.

3. FOIA Performance: The Current Situation

Currently, requesting and receiving information under FOIA is a highly particular process. Agencies responded to more than half a million requests last year, which presents plenty of opportunities to disagree with an agency decision or to criticize its customer service in a particular case. At a systemic level, there are three primary indicators that can be used to gauge the functioning of FOIA: processing, granting, and use of exemptions.

Earlier this month, OMB Watch updated our assessment and analyzed the fiscal year (FY) 2011 FOIA reports from 25 federal agencies, including most cabinet-level departments, and evaluated performance on processing requests, rates of requests granted, and the use of exemptions. OMB Watch reviewed the data from the latest FOIA reports along with similar data collected from FY 1998 to the present. This approach allows us to evaluate current performance in the context of historical performance.

Processing FOIA Requests

In FY 2011, the Obama administration processed more FOIA requests than in either of the two previous years of the administration. The 25 agencies tracked in the analysis processed more than 473,000 FOIA requests, an increase of more than 25,000 over the number processed in 2010, and *the highest number of requests processed since 2005.*

However, the number of requests received increased by almost 39,000, leaving 15,000 requests unprocessed at the end of the year. As a result, nearly one in five requests received in 2011 was not processed.

The Department of Homeland Security (DHS) is primarily responsible. In 2011, it received 36 percent of all FOIA requests. The number of FOIA requests DHS received rose to 175,656 in FY 2011 from 130,098 the previous year, an increase of 35 percent. Even though DHS increased the absolute number of requests it processed, the department was unable to keep up with the increased number of FOIA requests coming in.

The Obama administration placed a high priority on reducing backlogs of FOIA requests and in the Open Government Directive called on agencies with significant backlogs to reduce them by 10 percent per year.[5] Fourteen of the 25 agencies examined had fewer than 1,000 FOIA requests awaiting processing at the end of FY 2010. Of the 11 agencies with more than 1,000 requests backlogged in FY 2010, five have reduced the number of unprocessed requests by more than 10 percent from the previous years (the State Department, Environmental Protection Agency, Department of Agriculture, Department of Defense, and Department of the Interior). The State Department slashed its backlog by almost 60 percent in one year, dropping from just over 21,000 requests pending in FY 2010 to around 8,700 unprocessed requests in FY 2011. Two more

---

[5] Peter R. Orszag, "Open Government Directive," Office of Management and Budget, Dec. 8, 2009, http://www.whitehouse.gov/sites/default/files/omb/assets/memoranda_2010/m10-06.pdf.

agencies reduced their backlogs but by less than 10 percent – the Department of Justice and Department of Transportation. In the remaining four agencies with more than 1,000 unprocessed requests in 2010, the backlog rose in 2011 – the Department of Homeland Security (35 percent), the Department of the Treasury (eight percent), the National Archives and Records Administration (13 percent), and the Equal Employment Opportunity Commission (16 percent).

Granting FOIA Requests

Not all requests for information are actually granted. In terms of granting public information to those requesting it, the Obama administration's combined average (95 percent) is higher than the average of the Clinton administration (89 percent) and the Bush administration (93 percent). Our analysis excluded requests that have been denied for reasons other than exemptions, such as information requested from the wrong agency or requests for which no records were found. Thus, if a FOIA request is processed, the Obama administration is very likely to fulfill at least part of that request. However, the Obama administration is more likely to only partially grant the requested information (i.e., some portion of requested records are withheld) than the previous two administrations: the Obama administration partially granted information in 50 percent of FOIA requests, compared to 30 percent for the Bush administration and 17 percent for the Clinton administration.

Use of Exemptions

Under FOIA, there are nine reasons why agencies can deny a request. In FY 2011, total use of exemptions dropped by seven percent. The changes in the use of particular exemptions, however, tell a more complicated story. Although the exemptions are specified by law, agencies must use their judgment in whether to apply an exemption.

Two are seen as particularly open to discretion: exemption 2 (the interagency rule) and exemption 5 (the interagency memo). Under these exemptions, the agency claims that giving up information would "harm government functioning" but admits the information poses no risk to the safety or rights of American citizens. In FY 2011, the use of these exemptions dropped dramatically. Part of this was due to the March 2011 U.S. Supreme Court ruling in *Milner v. Navy*, which restricted the government's ability to invoke the interagency rule exemption.[6] As a result, use of this exemption fell by 63 percent. However, the decrease also appears to be the result of a deliberate policy change by the Obama administration. (The Bush Justice Department encouraged agencies to invoke these exemptions,[7] and their use ballooned.)

The "statutory" exemption was the fastest growing reason to deny information; its use increased by 64 percent, reaching the highest numbers on record. The bulk of this increase is due to a surge in usage at the State Department (for information relating to visa applications), as well as at the Equal Employment Opportunity Commission (for information relating to unlawful employment practices under the Americans with Disabilities Act).

---

[6] *Milner v. Navy*, 131 S.Ct. 1259 (2011), http://www.supremecourt.gov/opinions/10pdf/09-1163.pdf.
[7] U.S. Department of Justice Office of Information Policy, "New Attorney General FOIA Memorandum Issued," FOIA Post, Oct. 15, 2001, http://www.justice.gov/archive/oip/foiapost/2001foiapost19.htm.

Exemptions for personal privacy and law enforcement personal privacy remained near record highs. After growing throughout the Bush administration, their usage spiked in FY 2009 and dipped in FY 2010, but usage increased again in FY 2011. DHS is again the driving force behind the high use of privacy exemptions. It is unclear why privacy exemptions have grown so much over the years. It may be due to a significant change in the information being requested. However, some openness advocates are concerned that agencies may be stretching the scope of the exemptions to include records not previously considered to be covered by privacy laws.

OMB Watch believes that proper use of technology can significantly improve FOIA processing, bringing down backlogs, keep the level of granting requests high, and help establish consistent application of exemptions.

4. FOIA Portal: Spreading Innovation, Moving Toward a Centralized System

A key effort to use technology to improve transparency is the FOIA portal project being led by the Environmental Protection Agency (EPA). Although the project is still in an early stage, it deserves Congress' support. The project would scale up innovative technologies, already in use at some agencies, in order to significantly improve transparency and efficiency.

The FOIA portal project hopes to provide a single interface through which the public could submit requests to any participating agency, eliminating the need to find contact information for multiple agencies. EPA is heading up the project, in partnership with the Commerce Department and the National Archives and Records Administration. Other agencies are also welcome to join the project. The partners hope to launch the initial system this fall.

When completed, several aspects of the project would improve customer service and increase efficiency. The system would automatically assign tracking numbers to requests, which the requester could use to instantly view the status of a request, obviating the need to wait for manual replies from agencies. Agencies could also generate e-mails to requesters through the system to seek clarifying information or send invoices for fees, reducing mail delays and postage costs.

In addition, the project would aid agencies in improving processing in order to increase compliance with FOIA's statutory time limits. When an agency identifies records responsive to a request, it could add them to the system, making them easier to retrieve if needed again later. Consultations and referrals to other agencies could occur within the system, reducing the need to send documents around. The current consultation and referral process is a frequent source of delays and dead-ends for FOIA requests, so improvements in timeliness here would be very welcome.

The project would also bolster proactive disclosure, a key goal for E-FOIA reform. Released documents would be uploaded to a public website, and the requester would be notified of their availability. This critical feature would improve transparency by making released documents fully available to the general public, rather than delivered only to the requester. Withheld documents would remain in the system, restricted from public access but quickly available for agency review in the event of an appeal.

The project partners estimate the cost to build the system at about $1.3 million dollars, with an estimated annual operating cost of $500,000 to $750,000. To minimize development costs, the project will leverage the existing technological infrastructure of Regulations.gov, which already provides a common multi-agency interface to facilitate communication between agencies and the public. With full participation across the government, the agencies estimate the FOIA system would save a whopping $200 million over five years from improved efficiencies. In other words, a first-year investment of $1.3 million, followed by $3 million over the next four years (a total of $4.3 million over five years), could save the government an estimated $40 million a year in FOIA processing costs.

Congress has an important role to play in ensuring that these improvements to transparency and efficiency are realized. The portal's full benefits will only be realized when all agencies participate, and Congress should make clear that it expects every agency to allow requesters to use the system to interact with them.

While EPA and the partners are busy developing the system's core, the next step is preparing agencies to adopt the technology. In a time of budget contraction, a key factor will be to ensure that agencies have the necessary funding to cover the switching costs of adopting the system, such as training staff to use the new technology. Although we expect significant savings to be quickly realized from the new system, it will require a modest upfront investment from the adopting agencies.

Congress could also play a helpful oversight role in ensuring that the system maintains high standards of usability for the public. As with all e-government investments, the lead partners should continue to develop the system after its initial release, iteratively adding improvements to provide the best service to the American people. Through engaged oversight, Congress can support the best functioning for the system.

The administration also has an important role in ensuring the project's success. For instance, once the system is fully operational, the administration should direct agencies to utilize the multi-agency portal, as the Office of Management and Budget (OMB) did in 2004 in a memo directing agencies to use Regulations.gov.[8]

5. Additional Ways to Use Technology to Maximize Government Disclosure

In addition to the FOIA portal, several key reforms would strengthen the use of technology to improve transparency.

The Electronic Freedom of Information Act Amendments of 1996 (E-FOIA) was a key law for modernizing FOIA and increasing transparency. However, after 15 years of rapid technological progress, E-FOIA is showing its age. Updating E-FOIA for the 21st century could pay large dividends in improving government transparency, accountability, and efficiency.

---

[8] Karen S. Evans and John D. Graham, "Regulations.Gov," Office of Management and Budget, March 1, 2004, http://www.whitehouse.gov/sites/default/files/omb/assets/regulatory_matters_pdf/memo_pmc_egov.pdf.

Congress should strengthen the standard for publishing released FOIA documents online. Under E-FOIA, agencies must post released records that "the agency determines have become or are likely to become the subject of subsequent requests."[9] The current standard is vague and misses a key opportunity to expand online disclosure. Instead, agencies should be required to promptly publish *all* released documents, other than from requests made jointly under the Privacy Act.[10] Updating this standard would efficiently broaden public access to information.

In addition, Congress should expand the required types of information that all agencies must consistently post on their websites. Such requirements help reduce the number of FOIA requests by posting the information proactively. E-FOIA established some standards in this area,[11] but the categories of information need to be significantly expanded. The new list of categories should draw from the recommendations of the open government community's "transparency floor" and create a standard for transparency and accountability across agencies.[12] The information should shine a light on fundamental agency activities and strengthen public trust in government through disclosure. For example, agencies should:

- Post their FOIA logs and update them weekly;
- Post the calendars of department heads (i.e. Secretary and equivalent) and update them weekly; and
- Post their visitor logs at least monthly.

Additionally, Congress should consider setting a government-wide document proactive online disclosure goal (e.g., a total of 1 million new high-value documents online by the end of 2013). The Paperwork Reduction Act of 1995 established goals for eliminating unnecessary forms[13] and a similar approach could greatly benefit government transparency and FOIA. Such a goal would encourage agencies to think creatively about which documents represent the highest value. In the process, agencies should engage stakeholders, including FOIA requestors and website visitors, to gather input on which documents are the most sought after. The effort to meet such a goal would also force agencies to address many of the underlying technological issues such as electronic records management and document organization.

Congress should also expand on the tracking numbers it created in the OPEN Government Act by requiring agencies to provide status information online. Congress should also make clear that all agencies must allow the public to make and receive requests online.

Recognizing that proper management of electronic records is critical to any effort to improve FOIA through technology, Congress should update the E-Government Act of 2002.[14] Many of the current shortcomings of electronic records management are due to a failure to plan for information saving and sharing across government when new IT systems are adopted. Congress

---

[9] 5 U.S.C. § 552(a)(2)(D).
[10] 5 U.S.C. § 552a.
[11] 5 U.S.C. § 552(a)(2).
[12] The "transparency floor" or "openness floor" is a working proposal developed by the open government community for key types of accountability information that should be required on federal websites. See http://pogoblog.typepad.com/pogo/2010/08/new-item-in-openness-floor-ethics-program-reviews.html.
[13] P.L. 104-13.
[14] P.L. 107-347.

should direct agencies to consider full-circle transparency, including responding to FOIA requests, when making technology investments. Agencies need to ensure new IT systems will efficiently and effectively preserve and manage the public records they create, store, and transmit (and avoid acquiring proprietary systems that fail to address larger government record management needs). More thoughtful planning in the design of IT systems could save enormous amounts of staff time if systems were designed with a presumption of automatic disclosure. With a good, long-term IT strategy, the effectiveness and efficiency of the FOIA system could be transformed.

In addition to statutory reform, there are important steps that the administration could take to improve FOIA implementation and increase proactive disclosure. For instance, the administration is in the process of updating the policy for federal websites, which could embrace many of the important features for a modern FOIA system. The current guidance on federal websites, issued in 2004, does not articulate a vision of what agency websites are for or what agencies should seek to accomplish with their websites.[15] A new policy should explain that websites are a central method for agencies to offer information and services to citizens, broaden public understanding of what the agency does, and facilitate citizen participation with the federal governance structure. In particular, the new website policy should expand the information required on agency websites, including key information from the FOIA process and other types of information identified in the "transparency floor."

6. Conclusion

In conclusion, OMB Watch is fully committed to the Committee's goal of encouraging federal agencies to use the latest technology to comply more quickly and efficiently with FOIA requests and to proactively make government information easily available to the public. We believe that a common FOIA interface for the public, like the project being developed at EPA, has the best potential for achieving this result quickly. Recognizing the cost savings potential of such a system, as well as its democratic promise of a government more responsive to its citizens, we encourage the Committee to support the FOIA portal's success and broad adoption, including ensuring that agencies have sufficient funds to participate in a modern electronic FOIA system. In addition, other key statutory and administrative reforms could further strengthen the use of technology to improve transparency.

I sincerely thank you for the opportunity to address this Committee. Chairman and members of the Committee, I look forward to your questions.

---

[15] Clay Johnson III, "Policies for Federal Agency Public Websites," Office of Management and Budget, December 17, 2004, http://www.whitehouse.gov/sites/default/files/omb/memoranda/fy2005/m05-04.pdf.

Mr. KELLY. Thank you.

Again, everyone is right on time today within five minutes.

You made a comment in your opening remarks when you were saying the Administration answered it harshly. What does that mean?

Mr. MOULTON. Partial. I am sorry if I didn't pronounce it properly. Partial disclosures where a requestor would ask for a lot of documents or even one document and it might be redacted or some of the documents disclosed but not all and an exemption is cited to withhold some of that information, so a partial instead of a full grant.

Mr. KELLY. If I remember correctly, in the Clinton Administration, it was 89 percent, is that correct?

Mr. MOULTON. That is correct. That is a combination of both partial and full grantings. The Obama Administration uses a significantly higher partial granting as a percentage of that. There are about 50 percent of the grants they make or requests they answer are partially granted rather than full granting.

Mr. KELLY. When we talk about the information being answered, clear that up for me. You are saying that 50 percent are partially answered?

Mr. MOULTON. Right and then full granting would make up the remaining 43 percent. That combines to be a 95 percent average over the three years.

Mr. KELLY. Under the Bush Administration, it was 93 percent?

Mr. MOULTON. It was 93 percent combined.

Mr. KELLY. You are not running for office. You are allowed to make mistakes when you are talking to us. We are not going to film that and play it back later on.

So the Clinton Administration was 89 percent, the Bush Administration was 93 percent and now, under the Obama Administration, it is 95 percent. We have seen a marginal increase of about 2 percent. I know in 2008, you had some ideas that you submitted to President-elect Obama. Has a lot of it been taken in and placed into effect?

Mr. MOULTON. The recommendations we made during the transition had some impact. As Ms. Pustay testified, there have been a number of agencies that have been using technology more aggressively in opening up their online forms for requesting information. They call them portals.

The problem really is lack of consistency. Not all the agencies are creating the same types of capacity online and some of them aren't. We think the FOIA portal that EPA is developing really offers a level of consistency across government that is greatly needed.

Mr. KELLY. This portal they are opening at the DOJ, is it going to be similar to the EPA's? It sounds to me like the EPA has really done a good job with this portal as they come forward. I think you were talking about more of a partnership or a sharing. What do you see coming with that? Is it looking like it is going to merge? Are they going to have something very similar and as easy?

Mr. MOULTON. Certainly it is hard to say what will come about. I would say the features we know are being developed for the EPA FOIA portal far outstrip other portals and other efforts that we have seen from other agencies. It really is trying to put all of the modern advances and improvements that have been developed for FOIA in one place.

The FOIA portal that Ms. Pustay was talking about really was a portal to allow you to request information online, but I don't believe it has the same level of ability, it does have tracking but then to post the information to allow electronic communication.

Mr. KELLY. Mr. Moulton, thank you.

I am going to now yield to Mr. Connolly.

Mr. Connolly?

Mr. CONNOLLY. Thank you, Mr. Chairman.

Just clarify in response to the Chairman's last question, you are referring to the DOJ portal versus the EPA portal?

Mr. MOULTON. Correct. The DOJ portal is right now mostly just request information online. The EPA portal is going to be much more robust.

Mr. CONNOLLY. Right. So, Mr. Chairman, I think you were on to something there that would suggest the EPA portal really still could be a model even for DOJ.

Mr. MOULTON. Absolutely. Yes.

Mr. CONNOLLY. In response to one of the Chairman's questions, correct me if I am wrong, the statistic was something like 93 percent in the Bush Administration and 95 percent in the Obama Administration?

Mr. MOULTON. That is the average rate of disclosure, yes.

Mr. CONNOLLY. But what has to be taken into account in response to the Chairman's query is the difference in volume? Ninety-three percent of half a million is one thing; 95 percent of 1 million is quite something else again. Wouldn't we have to take into account the volume difference too, not just that percentage? It is more than a marginal increase if you take into account volume?

Mr. MOULTON. Compared to the last years of the Bush Administration, the volume is significantly higher. The Bush Administration did handle, in the beginning years when they took over from the Clinton Administration, a higher volume they dealt with for several years and requests steadily came down.

Mr. CONNOLLY. I am just saying the percentage may be a little misleading depending on the volume we are talking about. That is all.

I want to ask you three questions and I want to try to get them in 3 minutes and 29 seconds.

Uniform criteria, I think that is a good point you were making. We have 70 something agencies or 100 different agencies and they all have different criteria, sometimes they may have to given the nature of the specialized mission, but we ought to have some sort of universal criteria so we are all operating from the same playbook.

Are we making some headway in that regard, do you think? Is Ms. Nisbet's ombudsman role, her agency's ombudsman role, helping us in that respect?

Mr. MOULTON. I think we are making progress. We have seen a lot of agencies invest in technology, improve their processing, improve their proactive disclosure. It is partly comfort level, comfort with technology, comfort with FOIA, that leads some of the agencies to advance further and other agencies sometimes it is also a

resource question of having the resources to make those investments and improvements.

Mr. CONNOLLY. Again, we were talking about partial responses.
That can be, depending on one's point of view, a good thing or a
bad thing, a good thing in that at least you are trying to be responsive but you can't be 100 percent responsive for the exemptions or
privacy, whatever it may be.

On the other hand, partial may be no, you are not being responsive. You actually are kind of covering up and impeding transparency. What is your take on this increase in partial responsiveness by this Administration?

Mr. MOULTON. It is difficult to decide exactly what is going on
just based on the statistics. The increased use of partial disclosure
as part of the response from government has been growing for
many years since about the year 2000, growing steadily, more partial disclosures, fewer percentage-wise full disclosures.

This could be a change in government information. It may be
that government information is becoming more commingled with
privacy information or national security information, so partial
redactions are a necessity. It could also be a change in requests,
that people are requesting larger amounts of information and that
some of it is something that has to be withheld, or it could be, as
you say, a bad thing. It could be a change in the attitude and the
implementation by the agency.

From the statistics, it is impossible to tell. It would really require
an audit of requests, a random audit to see what was requested,
what was responsive and what was given to figure out exactly what
is going on here and driving this.

Mr. CONNOLLY. That is a good point. For example, maybe there
was a 1,000 percent increase in the Homeland Security requests. Of
course that is going to be a partial response if you are lucky. My
final question quickly is do you see a pattern of more or less
arbitrary barriers, obstruction, needless delays in the last few
years or are we improving in that regard?

Mr. MOULTON. You mean in processing FOIA?

Mr. CONNOLLY. Yes.

Mr. MOULTON. I think again the answer is that the record is
mixed. I think some agencies have made a lot of improvements in
removing preexisting barriers. I think that is something to also
stress that some of these barriers have been embedded in the process for years predating this Administration or the previous Administration.

Mr. CONNOLLY. It is a culture.

Mr. MOULTON. A culture of if it can be withheld, then it is better
to play it safe than sorry. That is something that is very hard to
overcome. There is a lot of training going on, a lot of investment
at various agencies going on, and I think some agencies have made
greater strides than others. We have seen some agencies who have
kept a more business as usual attitude towards processing FOIA
requests and having the same types of responses. Even when they
can disclosure more information, they choose not to.

Mr. CONNOLLY. Thank you, Mr. Chairman.

Mr. KELLY. Thank you, Mr. Connolly.

I would say whenever we talk about all this information that is out there, people are a lot more comfortable now. They are becoming more comfortable with technology, getting on and doing a lot of things maybe they wouldn't have done in previous Administrations, but also the world has changed dramatically after 9/11.

When I think what we put out there, I don't know another country in the world that allows more people to look at what it is doing. I would say our model is probably the most perfect model out there but it also does allow for an openness no place else in the world does allow and I do think we have to be very careful with it.

I would agree with Mr. Connolly, I think the world changing so quickly, the amount of information that is out there, we do have to be very careful with it. The President's opening remarks, again I go back to, sometimes we have to be careful. We open a Pandora's Box. We establish a standard that is may be hard to live up to in the real world. As we go forward, I think the public does expect, and may be more suspect, of things than they were before. We have a lot more people asking a lot more questions at a lot of different levels. While some people think that is very healthy, I do think it is healthy, but again, there is a lot of responsibility with how you handle that material.

I really do appreciate you being here today. All the panel members, thank you for what you are doing in service to our country.

With that, the meeting is adjourned. Thank you.

[Whereupon, at 4:30 p.m., the subcommittee was adjourned.]

STATEMENT FOR THE RECORD

COMMITTEE ON OVERSIGHT AND GOVERNMENT REFORM
U.S. HOUSE OF REPRESENTATIVES

March 21, 2012

*Hearing: FOIA in the 21ˢᵗ Century:
Using Technology to Improve Transparency in Government*

2154 Rayburn House Office Building
Chairman James Lankford (OK-5)

Mary Beth Hutchins
Communications Director, Cause of Action

Thank you, Chairman Lankford, for the opportunity to submit this statement for the record to the Committee on Oversight and Government Reform at the U.S. House of Representatives. My name is Mary Beth Hutchins and I am the Communications Director at Cause of Action.[1] Cause of Action is a nonprofit, nonpartisan organization that uses public advocacy and legal reform strategies to ensure greater government accountability and protect taxpayer interests and economic freedom.

One of the tools necessary for Cause of Action's oversight activities is the Freedom of Information Act (FOIA). While Cause of Action has sent numerous FOIA requests on a diversity of issues, I wanted to concentrate on Cause of Action's particular efforts to understand how (and ensure that) discretionary, non-contractual award programs in the federal government are competitive and merit-based.

The Federal Government Has Stonewalled Cause of Action's FOIA Requests

In many instances, Cause of Action has been unable to successfully use the FOIA process to inform the public about how our tax dollars are being spent by federal programs. Throughout its several-month-long investigation into federal discretionary grant spending, Cause of Action has learned that most federal government agencies lack the ability to track the documents associated with the awarding of these grants in an expeditious or efficient manner. Cause of Action staff has been told, for instance, that simply finding these documents and putting them together would take thousands of search hours alone.[2] Agencies have estimated that the costs of

---

[1] WEBSITE, CAUSE OF ACTION, *available at* www.causeofaction.org.
[2] *See, e.g.,* Voicemail Message from Eugene McGirt, FOIA Officer, Department of Housing and Urban Development, to [Rule 26(b)], Chief Counsel for Regulatory Affairs, Cause of Action, Mar. 13, 2012; Telephone

search, review, and duplication fees range from thousands to hundreds of thousands of dollars.[3] If the public wants to become educated about how their tax dollars are being spent, the current Administration is sending the message that it expects Americans to pay hundreds of thousands of dollars for that information.

Based on several telephone conversations with federal agency staff, after numerous attempts to get relevant records from FOIA, Cause of Action came to the conclusion that most federal agencies lack an internal audit process concerning discretionary awards, cooperative agreements, and loan guarantees. To illustrate this problem, Cause of Action asked the Department of Education whether there was an audit or examination process similar to the Internal Revenue Service's process for conducting an examination via the use of surveys and sampling and were told was that there was not.[4] Although some agencies or departments draft memoranda citing instances when an applicant received a grant out of rank order, this process was not incorporated into a system that could detect risk factors amongst grantees.[5] In other words, if a peer-review panel is overturned for political reasons, the agency has no way of flagging that event.

Because the federal government does not have processes in place for monitoring awards, Cause of Action has instead had to request the lists of all grants awarded and then study these grants for risk factors in order to then submit new FOIA requests for information.[6] If these lists are not provided per our request, the American public will be significantly limited in its ability to understand whether political favoritism has injected itself into the way tax dollars are doled out. Some agencies, such as the Department of Interior, requested that Cause of Action file separate FOIA requests to each of their offices because their discretionary grant process was decentralized.[7] Others, such as the Department of Energy, were able to provide us with a list of their discretionary grants over the prior three years, but had no way to search among those thousands of grants for the documents we requested.[8] Essentially, Cause of Action was told that the only way to do this would be to manually search through the data.

Cause of Action's FOIA Work on Administrative Earmarks

A recent study by the Heritage Foundation reveals that the federal discretionary grant process, for instance, can be used to engage in administrative earmarking, where taxpayer dollars are doled out by federal agencies for non-competitive, often political, purposes.[9] The

---

Call of [Rule 26(b)], Staff Attorney, [Rule 26(b)], Executive Director, Cause of Action and Alexander Morris, FOIA Officer, Joan Ogbazghi FOIA Specialist, Department of Energy, Feb. 22, 2012.

[3] *Id.*, Voicemail Message.

[4] Telephone Call of [Rule 26(b)], Staff Attorney, [Rule 26(b)], Executive Director, Cause of Action, James Hyler, FOIA Officer, Department of Education, and Corinna Zarek, Attorney-Adviser, Office of Government Information Systems, Feb. 22, 2012.

[5] *Id.*

[6] Email from Dorothy Lee, Office of the General Counsel, Office of Justice Programs, Department of Justice to [Rule 26(b)], Staff Attorney, Cause of Action, Mar. 8, 2012; Email from Eugene McGirt, FOIA Officer, Department of Housing and Urban Development, to [Rule 26(b)], Staff Attorney, Cause of Action, Mar. 15, 2012.

[7] *Id.*

[8] *See* note 2, *supra.*

[9] Lachlan Markay, *'Buying' House Votes for Unpopular Legislation*, THE HERITAGE FOUNDATION, (Feb. 22, 2012) *available at* http://blog.heritage.org/2012/02/21/morning-bell-buying-house-votes-for-unpopular-legislation/.

Congressional Research Service (CRS) has acknowledged that earmarking is conducted by the President and others in the executive branch during budget formulation and execution, "both at their discretion and through interactions with Congress."[10] CRS, in a report studying earmarks from fiscal years 2008 through 2010, determined that President Obama was disclosed as the "only requester" for 1,265 earmarks worth $9.5 billion.[11] The President and Members of Congress jointly requested 774 earmarks worth $12.4 billion.[12] 69 percent of all earmarks are either solely requested by the President or requested jointly by the President and Members.[13] CRS also determined "[b]oth the number and value of earmarks requested solely by the President increased since FY2008."[14] In fact, over this time, administrative earmarks increased 54%, from 819 to 1,265, while their value increased 126%, from $4.2 billion to $9.5 billion.[15] At the same time that the current Administration has increased its administrative earmarks, the number and value of earmarks requested solely by Members of Congress have decreased, "by 17% and 19% respectively, from 11,117 earmarks worth $12.5 billion in FY2008 to 9,281 earmarks worth $10.2 billion in FY2010."[16]

With the current Administration spending more on grant and loan guarantee-type assistance than on federal contracts, CRS's data confirms that there is a need for greater government accountability over our tax dollars in the area of non-contractual awards.[17] The American people have been outraged by stories of politicized loan guarantees like Solyndra and yet the Department of Energy is continuing to spend upward of $30 billion in loan guarantees while lacking the ability to efficiently manage federal funds and identify weaknesses in the loan review process.[18] Cause of Action is particularly concerned about how the federal government is conducting oversight over non-contractual awards, including discretionary grants and loan guarantees. Administrative earmarking takes place outside the Congressional appropriations process and the public has a right to know that its tax dollars are being spent in a competitive and merit-based fashion.

In December 2011, Cause of Action filed FOIA requests with 18 government agencies: the Departments of State, Commerce, Labor, Health and Human Services, Transportation, Justice, Interior, Housing and Urban Development, Veterans Affairs, Treasury, Agriculture, Energy, Education, Homeland Security, the Environmental Protection Agency, the Office of Management and Budget, the National Science Foundation, and the General Services Administration. Cause of Action sought documents relating to discretionary, non-contractual

---

[10] Carol Hardy Vincent & Jim Monke, *Earmarks Disclosed by Congress: FY 2008-2010 Regular Appropriations Bills*, CRS REPORT TO CONGRESS (R40976), Apr. 16, 2010, *available at* http://crs.gov/Pages/Reports.aspx?Source=search&ProdCode=R40976.

[11] *Id.*

[12] *Id. See e.g.* Fig. 4, Fig. 5.

[13] *Id.*

[14] *Id.*

[15] *Id.*

[16] *Id.*

[17] WEBSITE, SUMMARIES, USASPENDING.GOV, *available at* http://www.usaspending.gov/explore?carryfilters=on (last visited Mar. 19, 2012).

[18] U.S. GOVERNMENT ACCOUNTABILITY OFFICE, REPORT TO CONGRESSIONAL COMMITTEES, DOE LOAN GUARANTEES: FURTHER ACTIONS ARE NEEDED TO IMPROVE TRACKING AND REVIEW OF APPLICATIONS, GAO-12-157, (Mar. 2012), *available at* http://www.gao.gov/assets/590/589210.pdf.

grants that each agency had disbursed over the prior three fiscal years.[19] Because of the concern that federal grant-making could be used for political purposes, Cause of Action also sought communications relating to grant requests between the Office of the President and the agencies, and between members of Congress and the agencies. Cause of Action also requested documents and records relating to the review process used to determine which applicants received federal awards and whether there were instances in which agency officials overturned the decisions of a peer-reviewed panel.

The utility of FOIA as an oversight tool to track the federal government's activities is on the brink of being undermined. A recent Government Accountability Office report revealed the Department of Energy had severe deficiencies in its tracking of loan guarantees.[20] A March 19, 2012 *ABC News* story that assessed the struggles by both the Department of Energy and investigators from this Committee reveals a deeper problem that is evident to Cause of Action across the entire federal government: most agencies lack the ability to handle large amounts of information in a technologically savvy manner.[21] Given that hundreds of billions of dollars were given out through the American Recovery and Reinvestment Act (the Stimulus) over the past several years, it is surprising that government agencies are overwhelmed at the prospect of providing simple documents relating to their discretionary grants. Agencies have admitted that there is no electronic database that can be easily searched for specific types of documents.[22] Often documents are kept in separate offices, in paper format, and documents relating to a single grant may be dispersed through an entire agency in many different offices.[23] If a requestor seeks a single document and can pinpoint where that document would be, agencies seem to be able to handle that type of a request. But if a FOIA request asks an agency to produce records relating to financial transactions involving hundreds of millions of dollars, the complexity of the request immediately becomes too burdensome for the agency to handle. Worse, for a public interest organization like Cause of Action, it becomes the requestor's responsibility to audit grants and analyze risk-factors with spending – activities that the federal government should already be engaged in.

In response to the Heritage Foundation's study on administrative earmarks, White House press secretary Jay Carney continued to reiterate this Administration's "unprecedented" level of

---

[19] *See, e.g.*, FOIA Request of Cause of Action to Department of Health and Human Services, Dec. 7, 2011 (HHS-2012-0299GD).

[20] Lisa Rein, *Energy Dept. oversight on loans is inadequate, says GAO report*, WASH. POST, (Mar. 13, 2012), *available at* http://www.washingtonpost.com/blogs/federal-eye/post/energy-dept-oversight-on-loans-is-inadequate-gao-says/2012/03/12/gIQA04rX8R_blog.html.

[21] Matthew Mosk, *GOP Says Energy Dept. Cut Corners to Lend Az. Solar Firm $1.6 Billion*, ABC NEWS, *available at* http://abcnews.go.com/Blotter/gop-claims-obama-admin-cut-corners-arizona-solar/story?id=15950486#.T2dicvWy4cs.

[22] Email from [Rule 26(b)], Staff Attorney, Cause of Action, to James Hyler, FOIA Officer, Department of Education, Feb. 22, 2012.

[23] Letter from Ray McInerney, FOIA Officer, Department of Interior to [Rule 26(b)], Chief Counsel for Regulatory Affairs, Cause of Action, Feb. 8, 2012 ("[T]he actual administration of awards within the Department of Interior is very decentralized, and as such, information on awards and award recipients in maintained separately by each of the offices and bureaus within the Department. . . . Please submit your request for information . . . to the appropriate FOIA Officer(s). . . .").

"transparency and disclosure,"[24] by stating, "I'm confident that the issuance of grants through agencies . . . is done in a merit based way."[25] Cause of Action is particularly troubled by the Administration's response. On September 9, 2011, Cause of Action sent a FOIA request to the Office of Management and Budget (OMB) requesting records relating to efforts by the current Administration to ensure compliance with Executive Order No. 13457, which requires that communications from Members of Congress to the agencies regarding federal expenditures be made publicly available. Cause of Action's FOIA request dealt specifically with the issue of administrative earmarks and concerns that the federal expenditure process was not functioning in a merit-based way. OMB issued a letter, dated September 13, 2011, acknowledging receipt of Cause of Action's FOIA request and stating that OMB received our FOIA request on September 9, 2011. OMB sent a letter dated October 6, 2011 requesting an extension of "up to ten working days." On December 9, 2011, Cause of Action followed up by telephone to request information on the status of the FOIA request. OMB provided no such information.

As of January 11, 2012, OMB had not provided a response to Cause of Action's FOIA request. As of March 7, 2012, it had been well over the twenty (20) day statutory time limit for OMB to produce documents responsive to Cause of Action's FOIA request, even accounting for OMB's requested extension of time. Therefore, on March 7, 2012, Cause of Action filed a complaint in federal district court under the Freedom of Information Act, which provides a cause of action for an agency's failure to respond to a record request under 5 U.S.C. § 552(a)(6)(C).[26] As Cause of Action's lawsuit reveals, there is a clear disconnect between what the Administration is promising and what it is delivering in terms of FOIA.

Cause of Action respectfully requests that the Committee consider the inability of agencies to efficiently handle large FOIA requests, especially ones seeking documents relating to how agencies spend money for discretionary grants, as our organization has done. Thank you for your consideration of our views and experience with FOIA. We would be pleased to provide the committee with any further information the Committee requests.

Sincerely,

_____

MARY BETH HUTCHINS
COMMUNICATIONS DIRECTOR

---

[24] Matt Negrin, *Carney Defends W.H. 'transparency'*, POLITICO, *available at* http://www.politico.com/politico44/perm/0211/about_those_lobbyists_d25191cf-42da-4c47-9e08-2f558e246f1b.html.

[25] Nathaniel Ward, *Heritage's Markay Makes a Splash with His Report on 'Buying' House Votes with Federal Grants*, THE HERITAGE FOUNDATION, (Feb. 22, 2012), *available at* http://www.myheritage.org/news/heritages-markay-makes-a-splash-with-his-report-on-buying-house-votes-with-federal-grants/.

[26] Complaint, *Cause of Action v. Zients*, Case No. 12-cv-00379, (D.D.C. 2012). A copy of the complaint is attached to this statement.

Encl.   Complaint, *Cause of Action v. Zients*, Case No. 12-cv-00379, (D.D.C. 2012)